THE LIBRARY OF GREAT PAINTERS

DAUMIER

the whole history of painting.

LIFT PICTURE FOR TITLE AND COMMENTARY

HONORÉ
DAUMIER

TEXT BY

ROBERT REY

THE LIBRARY OF GREAT PAINTERS

HARRY N. ABRAMS, INC., *Publishers*, NEW YORK

Translated by NORBERT GUTERMAN
MILTON S. FOX, *Editor-in-Chief*

Library of Congress Catalog Card Number: 65-19225

CONTENTS

HONORÉ DAUMIER by Robert Rey   9

BIOGRAPHICAL OUTLINE   39

SCULPTURE, DRAWINGS, AND WATERCOLORS   41

COLORPLATES

THE PAINTER BEFORE HIS EASEL (Le Peintre devant son Tableau)

   The Phillips Collection, Washington, D.C.   *Frontispiece*

LAWYER READING A DOCUMENT (L'Avocat Lisant)

   Collection Dr. Robert Bühler, Winterthur, Switzerland   67

THREE LAWYERS IN CONVERSATION (Trois Avocats Causant)

   The Phillips Collection, Washington, D.C.   69

THE MOONLIGHT WALK (Les Noctambules)   *National Museum of Wales, Cardiff*   71

A CORNER IN THE PALAIS DE JUSTICE (Un Coin du Palais)   *Musée des Beaux-Arts, Lyons*   73

THE REPUBLIC (La République)   *The Louvre, Paris*   75

REFUGEES (Les Fugitifs)   *Collection Mrs. William Van Horne, Montreal*   77

EMIGRANTS (Les Émigrants)   *Collection Oscar Reinhart, Winterthur, Switzerland*   79

THE MILLER, HIS SON, AND THE DONKEY (Le Meunier, son Fils et l'Ane)

   Corporation of Glasgow. Burrell Collection   81

THE DRUNKENNESS OF SILENUS (La Marche de Silène)   *Musée des Beaux-Arts, Calais*   83

NYMPHS PURSUED BY SATYRS (Nymphes Poursuivies par des Satyres)

   Montreal Museum of Fine Arts. Miss Adaline Van Horne Bequest, 1945   85

"WE WANT BARABBAS" ("Nous Voulons Barabbas")   *Folkwang Museum, Essen*   87

RETURN FROM MARKET (Le Retour du Marché)

   Collection Oscar Reinhart, Winterthur, Switzerland   89

WOMEN AND CHILDREN UNDER A TREE (Femmes et Enfants sous un Arbre)

    Rijksmuseum H. W. Mesdag, The Hague   91

AFTER SCHOOL (La Sortie de l'École)   *Collection Alfred Daber, Paris*   93

THE BATHERS (Avant le Bain)   *Corporation of Glasgow. Burrell Collection*   95

LITTLE PEASANT GIRLS (Les Petites Paysannes)

    Collection Dr. Warner Muensterberger, New York   97

MEMBERS OF THE BAR (Membres du Barreau)

    Collection Mr. and Mrs. Charles Goldman, New York   99

DON QUIXOTE AND SANCHO PANZA   *Private collection, Zurich*   101

THE BEER DRINKERS (Les Buveurs de Bière)   *Collection Dr. Fritz Nathan, Zurich*   103

THE DRINKERS (Les Deux Buveurs)

    The Metropolitan Museum of Art, New York. Bequest of Margaret S. Lewisohn, 1954   105

THE DONKEY AND THE TWO THIEVES (L'Ane et les Deux Voleurs)   *The Louvre, Paris*   107

COUPLE SINGING (Le Couple Chantant)   *Rijksmuseum H. W. Mesdag, The Hague*   109

THE MELODRAMA (Le Mélodrame)   *Neue Pinakothek, Munich*   111

THE PRINT COLLECTOR (L'Amateur d'Estampes)   *Musée du Petit-Palais, Paris*   113

CRISPIN AND SCAPIN   *The Louvre, Paris*   115

CARRYING THE LAUNDRY (Le Fardeau)   *Collection Ernest Gutzviller, Paris*   117

THE FIRST DIP (Le Premier Bain)   *Collection Oscar Reinhart, Winterthur, Switzerland*   119

THE HORSEMEN (Les Cavaliers)   *Museum of Fine Arts, Boston*   121

THE WATERING PLACE (Baignade à l'Abreuvoir)   *National Museum of Wales, Cardiff*   123

THE WASHERWOMAN (La Lavandière)   *The Louvre, Paris*   125

MAN ON A ROPE (L'Homme à la Corde à Nœuds)   *Museum of Fine Arts, Boston*   127

FIVE SPECTATORS (Spectateurs au Théâtre)   *Private collection, Paris*   129

THE THIRD-CLASS CARRIAGE (Le Wagon de Troisième Classe)

    Collection Mr. and Mrs. David Bakalar, Boston   131

THE THIRD-CLASS CARRIAGE (Le Wagon de Troisième Classe)

    The Metropolitan Museum of Art, New York. Bequest of Mrs. H. O. Havemeyer, 1929.

    The H. O. Havemeyer Collection   133

MOUNTEBANKS' SIDESHOW (Parade de Saltimbanques)   *Private collection, Paris*   135

THE CHESS PLAYERS (Joueurs d'Échecs)   *Musée du Petit-Palais, Paris*   137

LUNCH IN THE COUNTRY (Fin d'un Déjeuner)   *National Museum of Wales, Cardiff*   139

THE TROUBADOUR (Le Troubadour)

    The Cleveland Museum of Art. Leonard C. Hanna, Jr., Collection   141

THE AMATEUR TRIO (Trio d'Amateurs)   *Musée du Petit-Palais, Paris*   143

TWO SCULPTORS (L'Atelier d'un Sculpteur)   *The Phillips Collection, Washington, D.C.*   145

MOUNTEBANKS RESTING (Saltimbanques au Repos)

    Collection Mr. and Mrs. Norton Simon, Fullerton, California   147

THE WRESTLERS (Les Lutteurs)   *The Ordrupgaard Collection, Copenhagen*   149

DON QUIXOTE ATTACKING THE WINDMILLS (Don Quichotte Chargeant les Moulins)

    Collection Mr. and Mrs. Charles S. Payson, New York   151

DON QUIXOTE   *Neue Pinakothek, Munich*   153

DON QUIXOTE AND THE DEAD MULE

    The Metropolitan Museum of Art, New York. Wolfe Fund, 1909   155

IN A PAINTER'S STUDIO (Dans l'Atelier d'un Peintre)

    Collection Mr. and Mrs. Norton Simon, Fullerton, California   157

PIERROT STRUMMING THE GUITAR (Pierrot Chantant)

    Collection Oscar Reinhart, Winterthur, Switzerland   159

SELECTED BIBLIOGRAPHY   160

h. Daumier

FOR MORE THAN HALF A CENTURY Honoré Daumier's irrepressible gifts held Paris spellbound. The public was delighted with his cartoons, which appealed to its dormant revolutionary spirit. And yet he was completely misunderstood—misunderstood by the public and probably also by himself.

1. Caricature of Daumier,
by Benjamin Roubaud (Benjaim). Lithograph

His immense output is most notable for the hundreds of lithographs he made to be sold individually over the counter. But all his life he dreamed of being in a position to give up lithography and to devote himself to his real passions—painting and sculpture. For this incomparable draftsman was a born sculptor. Diverted from the most deep-rooted of his gifts to painting, he was forever being diverted from it, too, by the need to earn a living. The wolf was never far from his door, and so time after time he was obliged to address himself to the lithographic stone and with good-humored resignation give the public what it wanted.

The fact is that he had a rather Bohemian notion of the artist as a nonconformist. From earliest childhood he had been poor, and as a young man he associated with rebellious art students. His life was one of insecurity to the very last, and it seemed natural to him that it should be so.

He was not much given to expressing himself in writing. It is possible to reconstitute the most important events of his career in their proper sequence, but his inner life presents more problems. To get at his private hopes and fears we have to study his individual works—the drawings, paintings, and sculptures—with special attention, as carefully as a doctor applying a stethoscope to a patient's chest.

*   *   *

Daumier was born in Marseilles on February 26, 1808, in a little shop on the Place Saint-Martin, which no longer exists. He was baptized Honoré Victorin. His father was Jean-Baptiste Louis Daumier, originally from Béziers. His mother's name was Cécile Catherine Philippe.

His father, a glazier by trade, was also an indefatigable scribbler of verse. France under the Empire was being fanned by many poetic winds, now elegiac,

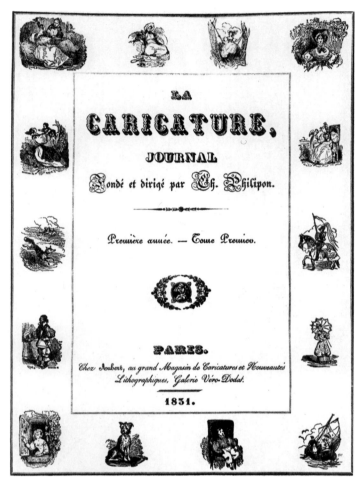

2. Cover of the first issue of *La Caricature*

3. GARGANTUA. 1831. Lithograph

now epic, and the glazier was sensitive to them all. In 1814 he packed up his manuscripts and took the stagecoach to Paris, leaving his wife and their six-year-old son behind in Marseilles. He was not slow to discover how hard and long a task it is to get one's literary gifts appreciated in the capital.

A simple-minded, hearty sort of man, a good father, and a sentimental if not always faithful husband, the elder Daumier missed his wife and son, who were leading a penurious existence in Marseilles. In 1816 he found a very minor post with the *Caisse d'Arbitrage* and sent for them.

Though Jean-Baptiste Louis Daumier never gave up his dreams of literary fame, he wanted his son to learn some trade which would make him self-supporting. Apparently in his eyes the process server was the very symbol of power and authority, for he made Honoré go to work for one of them.

At the age of twelve, the boy found himself in just the sort of sordid establishment which Balzac and later Dickens portrayed as the natural habitat of their most repulsive characters. Daumier fled as soon as possible—though he never forgot—this dismal milieu of legal documents and went to work for Delaunay, a well-known bookseller in the Palais Royal. But he did not stay long here either: his awakening passion for art was already too strong.

At this point the glazier-poet consulted his eminent friend Alexandre Lenoir, artist and archaeologist, who consented to keep an eye on the boy. His influence on the young Daumier was far greater than is generally thought and can be seen in several of Daumier's major works.

Not long afterward Honoré entered the Académie Suisse, an art school located on the Quai des Orfèvres, where the Palais de Justice stands today. Suisse was a former model, and in his establishment the students could make drawings from life; these classes were held first thing in the morning. There Daumier made friends with the painter Philippe Auguste Jeanron, an official of the Académie des Beaux-Arts for several months in 1848 and an exceptionally energetic and enlightened administrator.

Honoré Daumier had little in common with his father, a petty bourgeois who favored the restoration of the monarchy, and was in truth a dabbler as a poet.

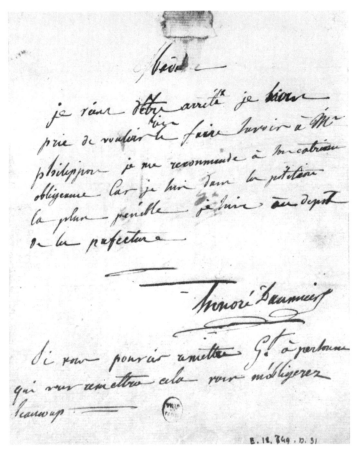

4. Letter from Daumier asking Mme. Philipon to inform M. Philipon of his arrest. *Musée Carnavalet, Paris.*

As is not uncommon, Honoré embraced opinions diametrically opposed to his father's. The inspirers of his political attitudes were working people.

Lithography at this time had become very popular, although less than twenty years had passed since this comparatively new medium was first used for the mass reproduction of drawings. Lithographic shops were springing up everywhere and prospering. This low-cost reproduction process was encouraging a new conception of art, an art for the man in the street. The stamp taxes kept the cost of newspapers beyond the reach of the common people; moreover, the majority of Frenchmen were still illiterate. Pictures alone could reach them, and the process of lithography now made this possible.

Daumier was quick to learn the technique. His teacher was one Ramelet, a painter and lithographer who is quite forgotten today, and Daumier's first lithographs were far inferior to the masterful works with which he amazed his epoch after 1830. They were street scenes, just good enough to keep him from starv-

ing. Even at this early date, however, it seems that Daumier was painting in his spare time. There is also reason to believe that he was already practicing sculpture. His cartooning talents asserted themselves in politically aggressive squibs directed at Charles X, the police, and the clerical party. These earliest cartoons were not signed.

La Silhouette, the first satirical weekly of its kind, was founded in 1829, just a year before the fall of the Bourbon monarchy. Its contributors were brilliant and irreverent. During the two years of its existence Ratier and Ricourt, the editors-in-chief, were twice arrested and tried. *La Silhouette* published three of Daumier's best early lithographs, including *The Old Flag,* an already remarkable work.

In 1830 came the revolutionary events of July 27, 28, and 29, "the three glorious days." Daumier's art will be better understood if we recall how intense were the political and social passions raised by the July Monarchy.

We look back at the reign of Louis Philippe as a peculiarly peaceful epoch, but in fact the regime labored under financial difficulties from the first, and there were many social disorders as well as disasters such as the outbreak of cholera, which in 1832 killed 22,000 people in Paris alone (among them the prime

5. Photograph of Sainte-Pélagie,
the prison where Daumier was held

6. SOUVENIR OF SAINTE-PÉLAGIE. 1833. Lithograph.
(The standing figure may be a self-portrait.)
Courtesy Bibliothèque Nationale, Paris

minister, Casimir Périer). The progressive parties did not fail to hold the government responsible for all such misfortunes. France lived in a chronic state of rebellion, and secret societies fanned the fires of discontent.

The moment Louis Philippe ascended the throne, his actions and attitudes began to toughen. For all that he had been King of the Barricades, he favored middle-class interests; the bourgeoisie looked upon him as a model for the nation to emulate. When he took stern measures against the agitation of the proletariat, it became more firmly rebellious. Measures of repression merely encouraged acts against the government.

We do not know what part Daumier had taken in the street fighting in July, but that his heart was with the revolutionaries is evident from his lithograph which portrays an "insurgent grocer" (fig. 12). In his eyes the July Revolution had turned out to be a gross deception. His most cherished illusions had been destroyed, and he never forgave Louis Philippe, now King of the French, for it.

Nor was it only leftists who opposed the king. On April 28, 1832, the Duchess de Berry landed at Marseilles in an unsuccessful attempt to replace Louis Philippe with the heir of the old Bourbon line, and there was an uprising later in the Vendée.

In this overheated atmosphere, artists (many of them among the best) who worked on the popular newspapers began to bombard the regime with cartoons. And of all the taunts and denunciations, Daumier's lithographs were the most deadly.

His art was inseparably linked with the existence of certain illustrated periodicals. Their origin and activity must be kept in mind if we are to grasp the meaning of the events which took place at the time.

Daumier might never have become Daumier without *La Caricature* (fig. 2). And *La Caricature* would never have come to be without Charles Philipon. This amazing man became famous among artists of the day for his droll caricatures. Seeing the growing popularity of the lithograph, he persuaded his brother Aubert, a former notary, to found with him in 1830 the Aubert firm of publishers. Their offices were in the Passage Vérot-Dodat, which even today maintains its colorful character.

Aubert and Charles Philipon launched *La Caricature* in 1831, three months after Louis Philippe had ascended the throne. From the outset it was violently hostile to the new regime. Very promptly it gathered the best of the militant young artists and writers. For Daumier, it was a chance to become famous almost overnight. The common people who had fought and won the revolution which put Louis Philippe on the throne soon understood that not they but the bourgeoisie were reaping the rewards. They did not take it lying down. There were terrible uprisings, and in Lyons, for example, bloody reprisals by the government.

Louis Philippe drew his principal support from the middle class, now promoted to the rank of foremost pillar of the regime. From wealthy bankers right down to the smallest retail merchant, every member of the class was being given an official token of esteem. Since the memory of Napoleon's military glory persisted, the best way to ennoble so many bureaucrats and shopkeepers seemed to be to make wholesale distributions of various insignia of the Legion of Honor.

Louis Philippe's disbursement of such distinctions right and left inspired Daumier's *Gargantua* (fig. 3)—a lithograph in doubtful taste and of inferior quality, but the one which more than any other made him famous. It shows a crowd of officials and dignitaries stuffing a gigantic Louis Philippe with tribute. He sits there like some greedy Buddha, with no less greedy members of his big family behind him—but the throne on which he is sitting is actually a closestool. An abundant shower of medals is pouring out of the royal fundament.

The government could hardly ignore this. *Gargantua* was published on December 15, 1831. On February 23, 1832, Daumier was haled before the *Cour d'Assises*, sentenced to six months' imprisonment, and fined 500 francs. At the time, however, he was not jailed.

* * *

Daumier became conscious of his vocation as a sculptor, or at least confirmed in his inclination, when he met Antoine Auguste Préault. Among all the younger sculptors he may have encountered in his early years, he must have felt closest to Préault. In Préault, a master of the rough sketch, he found exemplified a style that had about it nothing of the slick finish of the academic studios. Since Daumier intended to sculpt for his own pleasure only, Préault's uneven, impromptu style was in keeping with his aspirations and his needs.

There was a vogue for small terra-cotta statuettes, caricatural in style, emphasizing big heads on little bodies. The sculptor Jean-Pierre Dantan (called Dantan le Jeune) had had a great deal to do with making this kind of sculpture popular. He kept a shop at one corner of the Passage des Panoramas, and people crowded around the windows, identifying the figurines as this or that fashionable Parisian personality of the moment.

Dantan's success inspired Philipon to commission from Daumier, in April, 1832, a series of similar

7. THE LEGISLATIVE BODY. 1834. Lithograph. *Courtesy The National Gallery of Art, Washington, D.C., Rosenwald Collection*

13

figurines. They were to represent the leading deputies of the conservative party (figs. 55-61). Daumier must have studied his models by attending sessions of the Chamber, and then, while his visual memory was still sharp, rapidly worked the clay until it embodied sinister, obsequious little figures, smugly, sordidly selfish, obtusely sure of themselves. Like the shrunken heads of Peru, the effigies molded by Daumier are the enemy himself, reduced to his quintessence. The young magician (Daumier was then no more than twenty-four) put everything he had into these little lumps of clay: their plastic qualities go far beyond mere caricature.

Daumier executed forty-five such clay statuettes. Thirty-seven of them are still extant, though very fragile. Fortunately, bronze casts were made of them in 1925.

Dantan's figurines, however witty and clever, must have seemed dull beside Daumier's. Philipon exhibited the latter in the window of *La Caricature's* offices.

9. MR. BAILL.. (Bailliot). 1833. Lithograph.
Courtesy Bibliothèque Nationale, Paris

8. MR. GUIZ.. (Guizot). 1833. Lithograph.
Courtesy Bibliothèque Nationale, Paris

From then on there were always crowds in the Passage Vérot-Dodat.

*   *   *

Daumier, a prisoner in theory and a free man in actual fact, was making things harder for himself. He changed his signature to "Rogelin" for a time, but his increasingly trenchant style identified him unmistakably.

When he published a lithograph titled *La Cour du Roi Pétaud*, he succeeded in exhausting the government's patience. The police came for him on August 31, 1832, at the lodgings he shared with his parents. He was taken to the prison of Sainte-Pélagie. The first thing Daumier did in prison was to write Madame Philipon an account of what had happened, asking her to tell the editor-in-chief of *La Caricature* (fig. 4).

Although Louis Philippe did not hesitate to repress popular unrest with the utmost severity, he was not eager to make noisy martyrs of artists and intellectuals. This was why Daumier had been sent to Sainte-

Pélagie (figs. 5, 6), a prison notable for its indulgent treatment of "politicals."

Needless to say, Philipon informed his readers of Daumier's arrest, and rather melodramatically. He succeeded in persuading the authorities that the artist should serve his sentence in a mental hospital rather than in a prison. The transfer took place on November 11, 1832, so that Daumier spent only some seventy days in Sainte-Pélagie instead of the 180 days to which he had been sentenced.

Nor were the seventy days in jail very terrible. Daumier could exchange letters with his family as well as with Philipon and Jeanron. We learn from his letters that he was drawing a great deal and kept cheerful "just to annoy the government." The new drawings were not so inflammatory, but they still caricatured prominent figures of the Parisian bourgeoisie and the balls the king was giving at the Tuileries palace, currently referred to as "the chateau." He managed to get several of these drawings to Ramelet, who had them printed.

The political prisoners had plenty of leisure at Sainte-Pélagie. They talked a great deal. At sunset, there were "evening prayers" in the prison yard, when prisoners walked in procession behind a tricolor, singing republican songs.

Gargantua made Daumier very popular among his fellow prisoners. They always called him "Gargantua," occasionally adding to this nickname that of "Gouape" (i.e., "Hooligan"), no doubt because of his youth and his playful "art student" ways. *Gargantua* passed from hand to hand around the prison, and some of the cells had copies of the lithograph tacked up on the walls.

Daumier was released February 14, 1833.

*   *   *

When Louis Philippe came to the throne he had lavished every sign of affection on the aged Marquis de Lafayette, but there was little sympathy between the new monarch and the veteran liberal.

Lafayette had become the emblem of constitutional opposition. Old and feeble, he insisted on walking in the procession at the funeral of the deputy Dulong, a liberal whom Bugeaud had killed in a duel. It was his last public appearance.

Louis Philippe expressed no more than official regrets on the death of the old hero of the American

10. MR. KÉRATR. (Count de Kératry). 1833. Lithograph.
Courtesy Bibliothèque Nationale, Paris

Revolution in May, 1834. Daumier, in one of his compositions (inadequately characterized as cartoons), *Lafayette is Buried . . . You've Had It, Old Man*, shows the monarch in close-up, guffawing, his face concealed by his hands, while in the distance a hearse carries off his opponent's remains. This lithograph was the more effective because it came after the blow Daumier had dealt the regime on April 15, 1834, when he published *Rue Transnonain* (fig. 13). The constitutional monarchy was never to recover.

Serious riots had broken out in Lyons in the quarter inhabited by the *canuts* (silk weavers). The neighborhood had not forgotten the street fighting there two years earlier; the new unrest had, as before, economic rather than political motives. The silk weavers' wages had sunk to the point where they could no longer live on them. Workers received as little as ninety centimes for an eighteen-hour day. They went out on strike, and the government immediately invoked a law which specified such acts as a criminal conspiracy. Barricades went up all over Lyons, and the battle between the insurgents and the troops raged from April 9 to April 13, 1834.

The Lyons uprising had immediate repercussions in Paris. One whole quarter rose in rebellion on April 13 and 14. The Paris riots were marked by the most distressing confusion. The leaders of the liberal left, who had helped to fan the flames of revolt, soon felt that extremist elements were taking over. This frightened the liberals. Certain battalions of the National Guard, which had at first been favorable to the movement, reversed their stand. Well-known political figures who had been expected to provide leadership in the rebellion suddenly withdrew. The government minister Adolphe Thiers, for example, switched allegiance and ordered the suspension of *La Tribune*, the organ of the movement. Leaders of the Society for the Rights of Man were put under preventive arrest. The republican party was now a thing of shreds and patches. Lacking a unified command, what was to have been a revolution degenerated into mere street fighting.

In Lyons a handful of neighborhood section leaders erected barricades, blocking off several streets, including the Rue Transnonain. The government replied by mobilizing 40,000 troops with artillery, reinforced by National Guard units from Paris and its suburbs.

All this terrified the middle class. Most of the Na-

12. THE INSURGENT GROCER GIVES THEM A GOOD LOAD OF SHOT. Lithograph representing a street scene during the Revolution of 1830.
Courtesy Bibliothèque Nationale, Paris

tional Guard units and almost all of the regular troops hated the agitators. The breasts of the grocers and minor bureaucrats who made up the National Guard swelled visibly with patriotic conservatism and belligerence as soon as they donned their uniforms. The regular troops, meanwhile, were composed chiefly of rural illiterates, dedicated from their earliest years to the worship of money and property. They detested the urban proletariat as "collectivists" and "communists." The government could rely on such soldiers.

On April 14, before sunrise, the barricades in three Lyons streets, including the Rue Transnonain, were taken by the army. In the ensuing silence a shot was heard which seemed to come from an apartment in the Rue Transnonain. It allegedly wounded an officer, and touched off a wave of panic among the troops. They rushed into the building. Down dimly lit corridors they stormed, breaking into rooms with shutters still closed, stabbing with their bayonets at cupboards, beds, bed linen, and bodies—even firing point blank at mirrors in which they surprised their own images.

11. MR. SO-AND-SO, EUROPE'S LEADING CLOWN. 1833. Lithograph.
Courtesy Bibliothèque Nationale, Paris

16

Suddenly afraid of what they had done, they ran out of the building, their shakos rolling down the stairs after them.

And all was quiet once more.

Daumier's version of the incident shows the morning sunshine coming through the closed shutters, picking out patches of blood on the floor. Slowly, the light allows us to make out a pair of naked legs, a mattress spilling off a bed, the striped ticking under the torn pillowcases, bloodstains spreading over the marble mantelpiece.

Daumier succeeded in stigmatizing the horror of such an occasion for all time.

For it was a man of the people, a fellow human being, who had been murdered—the eternal sacrificial victim. The strength in those short plebeian legs—the nightshirt barely covers the thighs—had not saved him from the bayonet's thrust. The compact, solid body with its weight crushing a dead child is shown, blood still dripping from its nose.

Delacroix had already exploited the theme—the tragic immodesty of the corpse in a nightshirt—four years before, in a famous painting of the uprising of 1830 *(Liberty Guiding the People)*. Now, Daumier surpasses Delacroix in genuineness and immediacy of feeling.

* * *

Philipon was publishing a series of large prints in portfolios, separate from *La Caricature*. The collection had the overall designation of *Association Mensuelle Lithographique* (Lithographs-of-the-Month). Daumier's *Rue Transnonain* appeared in this series, as did others of his prints, including *Freedom of the Press* (fig. 14). Thus fear of judicial persecution did not prevent him from keeping up his pitiless caricatures of officialdom.

The constitutional monarch was a ruthless adversary, however, and the activities of the Aubert firm did not go unnoticed. Charles Philipon was spending more time in the prison of Sainte-Pélagie than in his office. Between 1830 and 1832 *La Caricature* chalked up

13. RUE TRANSNONAIN, APRIL 15, 1834. Lithograph. *Courtesy Bibliothèque Nationale, Paris*

14. FREEDOM OF THE PRESS. 1834. Lithograph. *Courtesy The National Gallery of Art, Washington, D.C., Rosenwald Collection*

seven trials and four jail sentences for its editor-in-chief. And yet the press kept on attacking the government just the same.

Ruined by heavy fines, *La Caricature* stopped publication in 1834. But at the very moment of its expiration, victim of the implacable judiciary, another publication, inspired by its example, was going into its second year. Scion of *La Caricature*, *Le Charivari* had been launched by Philipon in November, 1832, and in 1834 it carried on alone. After the suppression of *La Caricature*, Daumier joined the staff of *Le Charivari*.

At the outset the new journal had had the support of all the elements opposed to Louis Philippe—the extreme right-wing legitimists as well as the advanced liberals. In 1833, however, after criticism of the Duchess de Berry on the occasion of her secret marriage to the chamberlain of the king of Sicily, eight hundred subscriptions had been canceled. From that moment on,

Le Charivari was a purely republican organ, and at once the new publication became the target of efforts to suppress it.

* * *

Le Charivari fought the same fight as *La Caricature* and inflicted increasingly sharp blows on the regime in power. The response, of course, was increasingly harsh judicial measures. The police constantly discovered new revolutionary plots against the regime, some real, some provoked to demonstrate the vigilance and efficiency of the police.

Between July, 1830, and September, 1834, the government brought 520 lawsuits against various publications. The most violent leftist publication, *La Tribune*, was alone prosecuted 111 times, fined a total of 157,000 francs, and its editors sentenced to a total of forty-nine years of imprisonment.

On July 28, 1835 (the anniversary of the July Revo-

18

15. ROBERT MACAIRE AS A FINANCIER. 1837. Lithograph.
Courtesy Bibliothèque Nationale, Paris

lution), while he was reviewing the National Guard as it paraded down the Boulevard du Temple, Louis Philippe narrowly escaped assassination. Though the "citizen-king" was unharmed, several persons standing near him were killed.

Two months later the famous "September Laws" were enacted. They allowed the opposition press the alternatives of silence or the pretense of loyalty to the regime. The fine for giving any sort of offense to the king or for attacking the legal foundations of the regime was raised from 50,000 to 100,000 francs.

These new laws were so sweepingly and elastically phrased as to rule out any sort of criticism whatever. For example, it was forbidden even to mention the king's name in any discussion of the government. It was also forbidden to declare oneself a "republican" or to engage in public discussion of the principles of family, property, and sovereignty.

* * *

It was Philipon who discovered that the king's features

16. "JUST TAKE A LOOK
AT THAT FAT FIFINE. . ." 1840.
Lithograph. *Courtesy
Bibliothèque Nationale, Paris*

—the drooping jowls and the narrow forehead topped by a single upstanding tuft of hair—were pear-shaped. Naturally, the cartoonists were delighted with this discovery (fig. 11), for in vernacular French a "pear" is a dolt, a dumbbell, a "dope." Were an artist to be haled into court for merely drawing a piece of fruit, the judges and the authorities would look foolish. Thus Philipon's symbolic pear continued to be published even after the new laws had come into force.

Another artist's device to escape prosecution was to eschew the usual ways of drawing the king's features—i.e., in frontal view, in profile, or in three-quarter view. Daumier hit upon the unusual device of portraying the king in rear view. There could be no better proof that drawing, at least in Daumier's hands, can even express the unutterable. His figurations of a faceless monarch, seen only from the back, spoke far more eloquently than the conventional views.

Nonetheless, Daumier's development as a polemicist was undoubtedly slowed. Between 1835 and 1848, he was obliged to turn to less aggressive themes. It was in the course of these thirteen years that he produced the bulk of his more purely amusing drawings (figs. 16-24). Though his public never wearied of them, it

18. "GOODNIGHT, DARLING . . . IF YOUR GROCER HUSBAND COULD SEE US NOW . . ." 1842. Lithograph.
Courtesy The National Gallery of Art, Washington, D.C.

17. "I SAY, MADAM, I PREFER MY SOUP BALD." 1840. Lithograph.
Courtesy The New York Public Library

was a great strain for him to turn out enough of them.

Le Charivari during this period also reproduced some of his watercolors, for Daumier was again turning to painting.

*   *   *

Indirect means had to be found to ridicule the authorities, and Daumier hit upon a clever way to attack the commercial and financial chicaneries of the regime. This was the real sense of the many lithographs on the theme of *Robert Macaire* (fig. 15), which were published over a two-year period beginning August 20, 1836. Ostensibly, of course, they merely celebrate a timeless roguery: Robert Macaire is the confidence man, the trickster, the shady dealer par excellence. But in Daumier's handling of the theme, we have a full portrayal of the important role of business and finance in nineteenth-century French life, and how they became the real backbone of Louis Philippe's regime. Daumier's *Robert Macaire* was the dominant symbol of the century. What were the origins of the figure of Macaire?

On July 2, 1823, under the Restoration regime of the "legitimist" king, Louis XVIII, who was to reign for seven more years, the Théâtre de l'Ambigu (which specialized in low-life melodramas) produced a work titled *L'Auberge des Adrets* by Benjamin Autier, Saint-Amand, and Paulyanthe. In the course of the luridly melodramatic action, playgoers were introduced to a pair of desperadoes who had just escaped from a prison in Lyons—Robert Macaire and his confederate, Bertrand. At the Auberge des Adrets the bandits perpetrate a very nasty murder, the victim being the innkeeper. In the end, after a great deal has happened, they are unmasked. To exonerate himself, Robert Macaire turns on his friend Bertrand and puts all the blame on him. The latter replies by putting a pistol to Robert Macaire's head and pulling the trigger. As he dies, Macaire confesses his crimes. Curtain.

The leading role, that of Robert Macaire, was acted by the great Frédéric Lemaître, and it was his unforgettable performance in the role which really launched his career. How he prepared his extraordi-

20. "PARDON ME, SIR, IF I BOTHER YOU A BIT . . ." 1844. Lithograph.
Courtesy Bibliothèque Nationale, Paris

nary characterization is told by the poet Théodore de Banville in his *Recollections*. Although the poet was born the very year the play opened, he tells us what everyone in the theatrical world knew about how Frédéric Lemaître created the character of Macaire.

One day while the play was still in rehearsal the actor happened to be passing a shop (then just an open-air booth or stand) in the Boulevard Bonne Nouvelle, where a certain Père Coupe-Toujours made and sold *galettes* (a waffle-like biscuit or cookie). There the actor observed "a perfectly extraordinary creature, a kind of Don César of the sewers. His clothes were nothing but rags and tatters, but how magnificently he carried them off! On his head was a shiny top hat without any top to it. Around his neck was an enormous red scarf so arranged as to conceal the absence of a shirt. His waistcoat was filthy, but it had originally belonged to a dandy. It was green, and the buttons hung by a thread. He wore tightly fitting red army trousers, which had been cut off at the bottom with a pair of scissors. There were holes in his white stockings, and the satin uppers of his pumps had all but parted company from their soles. There was a black bandage over one eye. A pair of glasses dangled fop-

19. PYGMALION. 1842. Lithograph.
Courtesy The National Gallery of Art, Washington, D.C.
Rosenwald Collection

21

21. A RETURN OF YOUTH. 1845. Lithograph.
Courtesy The National Gallery of Art, Washington, D.C.
Rosenwald Collection

22. A DISTURBED NIGHT. 1847. Lithograph.
Courtesy The National Gallery of Art, Washington, D.C.
Rosenwald Collection

pishly at the end of a broad black ribbon. A twisted walking stick completed the getup. This creature stood there eating his *galette*, holding it daintily in fingers the tips of which stuck out of their gloves."

Frédéric Lemaître could not tear his eyes away until he had memorized every detail of the man's attire and demeanor. This was the basis of his creation of Robert Macaire.

Later, in collaboration with Benjamin Autier (one of the three authors of *L'Auberge des Adrets*), Frédéric Lemaître wrote a three-act play titled *Robert Macaire*, which opened at the Folies Dramatiques on June 14, 1834. It was a great success. In this reincarnation, Robert Macaire always stopped short of murder and was conceived as a rather attractive rogue who only took advantage of fools.

*   *   *

The government was prompt to grasp dangerous satirical implications in the play. The censors suspended all performances when the play had been running two months. Now Daumier took over. Philipon asked him for a series featuring Robert Macaire. For these lithographs Daumier left the captions to Philipon, who took

great pains composing them, and the arrangement led to a certain rivalry between them. Philipon thought he had as great a share in the popularity of these works as Daumier himself.

In the end Daumier produced no fewer than 120 lithographs on the theme. He was disgusted at the very fertility of his invention; he had less respect for the *Robert Macaire* series than for any of his other works. This was a mistake on his part. His pencil transmuted the legendary rogue into an important businessman. Dressed by the best tailors (whom of course he never pays), and living in a luxurious apartment (for which he pays no rent), Macaire is forever throwing dust in the eyes of the suckers he exploits, stealing from widows and orphans, pulling off confidence tricks in every class of society. Daumier's *Robert Macaire* has much in common with Balzac's *Le Faiseur*, but he is an infinitely more resourceful scoundrel.

At the time Daumier was producing his Robert Macaire drawings, swindlers were a highly topical subject. The age of Louis Philippe was full of get-rich-quick schemes. The West was then in process of mechanizing itself, with industrialization revolutioniz-

ing the crafts; economic theories and utopian dreams of a collectivist, humanitarian character were intoxicating a society that was giving birth to new organizational forms and looking forward to the future.

Concurrently with the Robert Macaire prints Daumier was turning out other work at a furious, exhausting pace: cartoons and amusing drawings of all kinds. He had to produce and keep on producing without letup. It is on this score that his life today strikes us as poignant. Once he had become famous as a cartoonist, there was no way of escaping the demand to produce cartoons. All his life he stole precious hours from his insatiable public to make paintings and sculptures, almost secretly, purely for his own pleasure and without hope of financial return.

charged atmosphere which gradually became even more tense. The inevitable explosion came on the night of February 22. Two political elements had prepared the event—one involuntarily, the other deliberately.

The first of these was the bourgeoisie. For some time it had been losing confidence in Louis Philippe. There had been an upsurge of the class's traditional anticlericalism and irreverence for the monarchy, and bit by bit the bourgeoisie had been drifting to the left. Its principal adversary was the minister Guizot (figs. 8, 55), who incarnated the resistance of the government to every effort at liberal reform of the constitution.

The other element was the self-declared republican party, frankly determined to overthrow the regime. It was well organized, and on February 24 showed it could move speedily. Once again barricades were thrown up all over Paris. The cry no longer was merely "Down with Guizot!" but "Long live the Republic!"

His paintings and sculptures, in conjunction with certain immortal lithographs such as *Rue Transnonain*, constitute the part of his work which today fills us with boundless admiration. And yet during his lifetime only a very few friends and art lovers paid the slightest attention to anything but his lithographs. Baudelaire himself, in his essay on Daumier, makes no mention of his painting or sculpture!

* * *

More than once Daumier repeated what Balzac had told him on a certain occasion: "If you want to be a genius, go into debt." He took this advice—moreover, in doing so he was merely following in his father's footsteps.

In 1842 Daumier had to contend with a certain Maître Fumet, a bailiff, in a matter of 110 francs, "the value of goods received" from a certain Braconneau. On April 14, 1842, he was notified that his furniture was to be sold off by order of the court. This kind of trouble was not unusual with him.

Daumier's life continued much as we have been describing it until 1848. The year opened in an over-

26. THE MARKET. 1848-50.
Black crayon and wash, $9^7/_8 \times 6^3/_4''$

27. DESTRUCTION OF SODOM. c. 1850. Charcoal, watercolor, and gouache. *Ashmolean Museum, Oxford, England*

On February 24, Louis Philippe was driven out of Paris, as thousands of Parisians surrounded and prepared to storm the Tuileries. The monarchy was a thing of the past—for the second time in less than a century. On February 25, France was once again a republic.

* * *

The republic! Daumier must have been carried back to the "glorious" days of the July Revolution in 1830.

On March 18, 1848, while public enthusiasm for the victory was still strong, artists were urged to compete in supplying the new regime with an allegorical figure to represent the new republic. Daumier planned to enter the competition and prepared a study entitled *The Republic* (page 75). Gustave Courbet, who was a hotheaded republican, announced that he would not submit a work in the competition because he wanted Daumier to win. In the end, however, officialdom called off the competition and Daumier never submitted the painting he had made.

A good deal had been going on in the time between March 18, when the competition was announced, and October 31, when Daumier's friend Bernard-Léon wrote scolding him for not having submitted his work. A tacit alliance between the extreme left and the monarchist opponents of the regime had indeed brought about the fall of Louis Philippe, but now conflict broke out between the two. Dominated as they were by opposing interests, they clashed openly during what became known as the "June Days." In the course of a four-day battle (June 23-26) an uprising by the working class was crushed. Accusations flew thick and fast between the conflicting parties, each accusing the other of slaughtering prisoners and finishing off the wounded. Some eleven thousand survivors of the uprising were sent to penal colonies, crammed together like cattle. Within a few months, the new and allegedly "republican" government had become so reactionary that it suppressed thirty-two newspapers at a single stroke.

The sect of the Saint-Simonians frightened the

28. COROT SKETCHING AT VILLE D'AVRAY. 1854-56.
Wash drawing, 14 × 10⅝″.
The Metropolitan Museum of Art.
Bequest of Mrs. H. O. Havemeyer, 1929.
The H. O. Havemeyer Collection

29. THE FAMILY. C. 1855. Black pencil and watercolor, $6^3/_4 \times 7^1/_2''$. *The Phillips Collection, Washington, D.C.*

bourgeoisie because it represented the communist ideal, though it was not really dangerous. Like the Phalansterians, the Fourrierists, and other utopians, the disciples of the Count de Saint-Simon seemed to Daumier not so much pathetic as grotesque. He had no sympathy with the brutality of the populace. In *Le Charivari* for March 4, 1848, appeared his *Paris Street Urchins in the Tuileries*. One of the urchins is shown sprawling on the throne. In the issue for May 5 he took the communists as his target. Just before the June massacres, extremists had hurled paving stones at the windows of *Le Charivari*, presumably protesting Daumier's lithographs. He was now forty years old. With age and experience, he may have lost some of his militant ardor of 1830.

In his satire *The Vésuviennes*, Daumier made a target of feminists, who were vociferously demanding "sexual equality"; and the *Divorceuses*, who were clamoring for reform of the marriage laws, were another target. Such agitation struck Daumier as absurd; he could only see the comic side. In his attitude toward these causes he was falling a bit behind the times.

After the June battles there were many men whose republican loyalties were beyond suspicion (Jeanron, for example) who did not feel obliged to resign their posts in protest.

Jeanron, newly appointed head of the national museums, passed on to his friend Daumier (September 19, 1848) a letter from Charles Blanc, a high official of the Beaux-Arts. The letter informed Daumier that the Ministry of the Interior was commissioning a painting and asked that he submit a subject of his own choice for official approval.

Daumier, who was always casual with deadlines, gave no thought to the matter for a long time. Actually, the matter was left in abeyance until 1863—that is, fourteen years later. To settle it once and for all, it was eventually decided that Daumier had acquitted himself with regard to the government by delivering to the Beaux-Arts a big gouache drawing, *The Drunkenness of Silenus* (page 83), which he had exhibited at the Salon of 1860.

It seems that Daumier was more bothered than pleased by this commission which specified no subject. The Rijksmuseum in Amsterdam has a large sketch signed "h. D." representing Christ instructing the disciples. Could this have been an effort toward filling the commission? One is tempted to ask the same question concerning another work, in grisaille on canvas, titled *"We Want Barabbas"* (page 87).

*   *   *

Daumier had no difficulty in recognizing the old objects of his contempt in the beneficiaries of June, 1848. There was still plenty to stigmatize; indeed, the tribe had increased. Though Daumier seems to have felt little sympathy for the new extremists in working clothes, he felt even less for *les ventres dorés* ("the golden bellies") of the Second Republic.

In 1849, the Chamber of the Republic (not a very democratic body) itself inspired him as subject of a new series, called *The Representatives Represented*.

Daumier saw clearly that the days of the Second Republic were numbered. In the not-too-far distance he heard the sound of marching boots. The country was ripe for the Second Empire, and this was one of the times when Daumier was moved to prophetic warning, embodied in *Ratapoil* (fig. 53).

Ratapoil is a monstrous, scrawny, bearded figure who evokes the ragtag and bobtail of the mercenary legions of the first Napoleon, half-starved, their pay forever in arrears. As an agent of the secret police, he scours the provinces. Discharged from the army for theft, he becomes a hero in the troubled atmosphere of the times: a shady figure who passes for a respectable citizen, an ex-convict who pats a judge on his fat paunch as he urges him to vote for the official candidate. Never before had insolence, ignominy, hunger, and vice been more compactly fused than in the clay figurine Daumier fashioned, which had to be kept from public view for a long time.

30. A GOOD BOTTLE.
1856–60. Pen and ink,
and watercolor,
$8^{1}/_{4} \times 11^{1}/_{4}$".
*National Museum,
Stockholm*

Ratapoil expressed Daumier's condemnation of the Caesarism fostered by the pseudo republic of 1848. When the historian Michelet saw the figurine, he called on Daumier and—so we are told—embraced him on his knees. In lyrical terms he celebrated the "artist," the "draftsman," the "thinker," the "lover of justice," whose immortal *Ratapoil* "has pilloried the Bonapartist idea for all time to come." It is probable that from this time on Michelet wrote Daumier's captions, for Daumier himself hardly ever bothered to supply them for his drawings.

* * *

A number of other works Daumier produced in these same years (1848-51) seem to us far more mysterious in character and on a higher plane. They represent some sort of migration of peoples and animals. Designated collectively by the title "The Emigrants" (pages 77, 79), the most remarkable single work among them is a sculpture (figs. 64, 65).

Daumier was now at the peak of his fame. Notable and talented men held it an honor to call themselves his friends. Balzac's words comparing him to Michelangelo were frequently repeated. Courbet, a believer in his own genius, proclaimed Daumier a great master. The independent younger painters, as yet unknown and often in straitened circumstances, who were soon to constitute the so-called Barbizon School, with Millet at the head, were warmly admiring. Decamps, then a very popular artist, praised the unique solidity of his drawing. Delacroix wrote to him in a tone of profound respect and copied some of his "bathing women." Gavarni never treated him as a rival, but openly admired the quality of a modeling which could dispense with such artifices as shading and scraping. Finally, Baudelaire found him so understanding a friend that his company became indispensable to the poet.

Living as he did on the Ile Saint-Louis, Daumier was

31. THE THREE GOSSIPS. c. 1860. Watercolor, $10^1/_4 \times 7^1/_8$″.
Courtesy Wildenstein & Co., Inc.

32. THE BLACKSMITH. Pencil, India ink, and gouache,
$13^3/_8 \times 9^1/_2$″. *Collection Claude Roger-Marx, Paris*

a near neighbor of the painter Boissard de Boisdenier, who occupied a sumptuous apartment in the Hôtel Lauzun, where Baudelaire had attic rooms. The most prominent Parisian artists and writers met there, and Daumier was accepted by them as one of the most distinguished men of the day.

It would seem, however, that his own preference was for simpler, less refined company. When he left the elegant gatherings at Boissard de Boisdenier's he would go to some cheap *café* where he could put his elbows on the table, wine-stained though it might be. One reason, perhaps, was that for all his fame he clung to his old, sloppy habits; after all, he was never free from the necessity of earning his own living as draftsman and lithographer.

LEFT:
33. THE BUTCHER. c. 1860. Watercolor, gouache, and pen, 11 × 9¹⁄₈″. *The Fogg Museum of Art, Harvard University, Cambridge, Massachusetts. Alpheus Hyatt Fund*

34. A LAWYER PLEADING. c. 1845. Pen and ink and watercolor over charcoal, 8 × 9″. *Boymans-Van Beuningen Museum, Rotterdam*

35. STREET CIRCUS. C. 1865.
Black pencil, watercolor,
and sanguine, 10³/₈ × 14¹/₄″.
The Louvre, Paris

36. THE MOUNTEBANKS. C. 1868.
Pen and ink, black chalk, wash,
and watercolor, 13¹/₄ × 15⁵/₈″.
*Victoria and Albert Museum,
London*

37. ORGAN-GRINDER. C. 1860. Black chalk, pen, and watercolor, 13³/₈ × 10¹/₄″. *Musée du Petit Palais, Paris*

Decidedly, Daumier could not live by painting, especially as he had married Alexandrine Dassy in 1846. Again and again he had to turn back to lithography to keep their heads above water. In 1852 he executed fifty-five lithographs, which brought him an average of 625 francs a month. It was a considerable sum, but Daumier never learned to save money.

In 1853 and 1854 he made several excursions to Valmondois, where he came to know Millet and Théodore Rousseau, who were painting there with Corot. In the following two years he executed more lithographs, and painted whenever he could.

In 1857 he produced a hundred lithographs, but he was becoming increasingly tired of this kind of work. He treated, or was made to treat, the most trivial subjects drawn from current life. In 1858, though ill and more exasperated than ever with what he was doing, he published eighty lithographs. On occasion he completed as many as eight stones in a single week.

38. TWO LAWYERS. C. 1850. Black chalk and watercolor, 8⁵/₈ × 6³/₈″. *Musée des Beaux-Arts, Reims*

Between 1848 and 1851 he painted a great deal, but in a way peculiarly his own. He would sketch a new idea on the canvas, and then try it again in as many as twenty different ways. This would go on until he was satisfied. The actual execution would take only a couple of days, and once he had completed the painting, he rarely went back to it again. He had to have the feeling that he had expressed the gist of his inner vision.

After the *coup d'état* of December 2, his whole life changed. His reputation as a revolutionary cartoonist scarcely brought him favor in the eyes of the new regime. Louis Philippe had sincerely appreciated the cartoons by Daumier which made fun of him, but Napoleon III lacked the other ruler's sense of humor.

Daumier exhibited at the official Salon (there was only one at the time, and until 1863 it was held every other year, sometimes every three years). One of his earliest paintings on the theme of Don Quixote was sent to the Salon. Cervantes' hero was to inspire Daumier to several immortal works.

39. THE ADVOCATE. C. 1860.
Black pencil, pen, and watercolor, $7^7/_8 \times 11^3/_8$".
The Corcoran Gallery of Art. W. A. Clark Collection

By 1860 these chores were all the more distasteful to him because he felt that his painting was reaching a high degree of maturity and beauty. It is from this period that those incomparable masterpieces, *The Drinkers* and *The Washerwoman*, date (pages 105, 125).

The canvases were piling up in his studio. Among them was a *Repentant Magdalen*. This had been commissioned late in 1848. He had received advances on it, and the final payment was made in May, 1849. However, the picture remains a sketch—he never finished it.

The canvases he exhibited at the Salon during these years remind us of Rubens in their treatment and coloring—*The Miller, His Son, and the Donkey; The Drunkenness of Silenus;* and *Nymphs Pursued by Satyrs* (pages 81-85). They did not go altogether unnoticed, but very nearly.

Was he distressed by this comparative lack of recognition? We do not know. It is not easy to divine what was going on in him. Perhaps he considered it profitless to dwell on his disappointments.

Meanwhile, everyone around him knew that his material situation was very insecure, to such a point that Gavarni proposed that he should contribute to *Le Temps*. But Daumier's thoughts were fixed wholly on painting now, and he rejected the offer.

It was a rash thing to have done. The public, feeling that he was increasingly aloof from it, that he was no longer trying to amuse it, lost interest in him. He began

to fall into disfavor. *Le Monde Illustré* stopped asking him for prints. Philipon himself, the friend and patron of the heroic period, put the blame on the fickleness of the general public, but he also recognized that Daumier's powers of invention were waning.

He was dealt a particularly cruel blow in 1860, when *Le Charivari* informed him that it would no longer take his lithographs. Daumier before long found himself in really straitened circumstances. The loyalty of his friends, however, comforted him. Unable to sell his paintings, he gave them away—*The Print Collector* to Corot, *The Drinkers* to Daubigny.

His friends did what they could to help. Michelet obtained for him a commission from the *Magasin Pittoresque*. Théodore Rousseau bought one of his paintings for fifty francs. The photographer Carjat, who was anything but rich himself, gave him three louis, "all I could afford."

40. GRAND STAIRWAY IN THE PALAIS DE JUSTICE. C. 1864.
Black crayon, pen, Chinese ink wash, and watercolor,
$14^1/_8 \times 10^1/_2$". George A. Lucas Collection,
Maryland Institute, Baltimore.
Courtesy The Baltimore Museum of Art

41. AT THE PETIT PALAIS.
c. 1840. Pen, pencil,
watercolor, and gouache,
$5^7/_8 \times 8^5/_8''$.
*Musée du Petit Palais,
Paris*

42. LAWYER AND CLIENT.
c. 1865. Watercolor,
$6^1/_4 \times 10^1/_4''$.
*National Museum of Wales,
Cardiff*

43. IN CHURCH. C. 1860. Oil on panel, 6 × 8⅝".
*The National Gallery of Art, Washington, D.C.
Rosenwald Collection*

Daumier, meanwhile, canvassed the dealers, offering pen drawings touched up with watercolor at fifty francs apiece. He did not find many takers.

His material situation grew worse and worse. In December, 1862, he had to sell some of his furniture. He left the Ile Saint-Louis and moved to lodgings in Montmartre; for a time his friends lost sight of him. But *Le Charivari* was discovering how hard it was to replace Daumier, and in 1864 offered him a new contract. It was a return to the public eye, and a banquet was given to celebrate it. Daumier realized that he still had many admirers.

In the same year, 1864, he produced about a hundred lithographs, which brought him in 400 francs a month. But he had no time for painting and sculpture.

Still, the public attitude toward him was changing. Connoisseurs were beginning to collect his watercolors. Surprisingly, the artist (who had always been a freethinker) set out to treat a religious subject. He completed an Assumption of the Virgin.

In 1865 Daumier left Montmartre. He did not go back to the Ile Saint-Louis, but rented a modest house at Valmondois. From 1866 on, his output of lithographs dropped to seventy a year, for which he got about 200 francs a month. He was fifty-eight years old in 1866, and his eyesight was beginning to fail. It was the year of the Prussian victory over the Austrians at Sadowa, and from that moment on Daumier sensed the approach of the ultimate disaster—war. More and

more his lithographs intimated the impending menace of death and destruction.

By 1868 his eyesight was growing poorer and poorer. Lifelong friends and colleagues were dying off. He had difficulty paying his rent at Valmondois and feared eviction. Then one morning he received the following letter from Corot:

Dear old comrade: I had a little house at Valmondois, near Isle-Adam, which was of no use to me. It occurred to me to offer it to you, and finding this was a good idea, I had it registered with the notary. It's not for your sake I am doing this, but to annoy the landlord.   Yours, Corot

Of this magnificent gesture Daumier himself said that he would not accept it from anyone but Corot.

He continued to exhibit at the Salon. In 1869 he entered a number of canvases, including *The Judges (Les Juges)*, *The Physicians (Les Médecins)*, and *The Amateurs (Les Amateurs)*. All of these were more than ten years old. That same year the Empire was prepared to award him the medal of the Legion of Honor, but

44. HIPPOLYTE LAVOIGNAT. C. 1860. Oil on canvas,
18¼ × 15". *The National Gallery of Art, Washington, D.C.
Chester Dale Collection*

45. INTERMISSION. 1858. Watercolor, 10⁵/₈ × 13³/₄″. *Kunstverein, Winterthur, Switzerland*

Daumier declined the honor quietly but firmly. He did not believe it would be in keeping with his long career as an independent critic of successive regimes.

1870: the Franco-Prussian war . . . Sedan . . . the fall of Napoleon III . . . the founding of the Third Republic . . .

Daumier, who now lived in Valmondois all year round, had been following sadly the stages of a debacle which came as no surprise to him. On November 16, 1870, he executed a remarkable lithograph, *Prometheus in Chains*, the perfect symbol of a France martyred in defeat.

During the war, when the newspapers did not publish, Daumier was threatened with destitution. On August 10 he signed a promissory note for 500 francs, and on August 29 another for 250 francs. In 1871, year of the Paris Commune, things were no better for him. In 1872, he executed the masterly

drawing which was to serve for his famous poster of the coalyards, *Entrepôts d'Ivry*. He was getting ever deeper into debt. In April, 1873, he gave a friend 100 francs as part payment on the 1,000 francs he owed him.

What did the Third Republic do for this long-time defender of republican liberties? It granted him a pension of 200 francs a month, which was later increased to 400. He was again offered the medal of the Legion of Honor, and once again declined it, as he had declined it under the Second Empire. Early in 1878 his friends and admirers organized an exhibition at the Durand-Ruel Gallery which comprised an imposing selection of his works. It had not been an easy exhibition to assemble, for Daumier's inveterate carelessness was still such as to anger even those who were at pains to make the exhibition a success.

Daumier's art now could be seen for what it was—

46. THE FIRST-CLASS CARRIAGE.
1864. Watercolor, $8^1/_8 \times 11^3/_4$".
*The Walters Art Gallery,
Baltimore, Maryland*

47. THE CRITICS. C. 1860.
Watercolor, $14^5/_8 \times 18^1/_4$".
*Montreal Museum of Fine Arts.
Bequest of Mrs. W. R. Miller
in memory of her husband,
William R. Miller, 1951*

48. THE AMATEUR. C. 1865. Watercolor, $17^1/_8 \times 13^3/_4$".
The Metropolitan Museum of Art.
Bequest of Mrs. H. O. Havemeyer, 1929.
The H. O. Havemeyer Collection

Daumier has registered sympathy for the old man who, from his window, sees an attractive feminine silhouette walking alone in the distance. There is sympathy, though Daumier makes fun of him at the same time. Did he especially long for the company of women? There is nothing to prove it. He was no doubt a good husband, and apparently treated his wife, "Didine," with hearty affection. But he would not have been appalled at the thought of a solitary life—note the lithographs on the subject of the bachelor. Where eroticism is concerned, he invariably notes only the ridiculous, extreme aspects.

What, then, is the place held by woman in his works? The charmer, the beauty, the temptress—Daumier rarely depicts her. It is only when he represents woman in her most natural context, that is to say, as inseparable from the child, that he treats her with extreme gravity.

In this connection, one of his most majestic compositions is *Soup* (fig. 73). Posed sideways, the seated mother is eating her food with great concentration. By the extraordinary alchemy of the maternal body, she is at the same time communicating the food as milk to the tiny person held at her big breast.

This man who was never a father (or rather, but once and then not for long), whom the figure of the

an enormous body of work. Public opinion was deeply impressed. Yet the exhibition did not make expenses—far from it. Nonetheless, Daumier had at last to be recognized as something far more than a mere cartoonist. He could now sit and smile in the silvery sunshine of Ile de France, his wrinkled old face framed by his white beard and great mane of white hair.

He died at Valmondois on February 11, 1879.

*   *   *

Today, in the perspective of time, we can catch deeper glimpses into the soul of this artist of genius. Although he seemingly lived out his life in full public view, on closer examination we must recognize that he gave away far fewer secrets than most of his contemporaries. For one thing, was he subject to the most exacting of the passions that stir the human soul—carnal love? It does not seem so. Contemporaries of the artist have given us to understand that for a very short period in his life he was prey to the torments of love. But we find little trace of it in his works.

49. LOOKING AT A LITHOGRAPH BY RAFFET. C. 1865.
Watercolor, $10^1/_4 \times 12^1/_4$". *The Louvre, Paris*

37

child alone inspired rarely, became emotional almost to the point of tears whenever the small one was caught up in the affections of an adult.

* * *

Surveying Daumier's immense output we must observe that, like Molière and Daumier's contemporary, the writer Courteline, he is the very opposite of a dispenser of gaiety. He is too rational not to recognize that the beggar may be a lazy fraud, but at heart he believes deeply that poverty is a terrible misfortune. Heart and head go together to produce drawings which portray the human condition in well-nigh tragic accents.

What overall impression emerges from the collection of lithographs, paintings, and sculptures produced by Daumier's busy hands over a lifetime in which leisure was so rarely his? An impression that the real Daumier is to be found in the few works which reveal

51. Caricature of Daumier, by Etienne Carjat. Lithograph. *Courtesy Bibliothèque Nationale, Paris*

50. Photograph of Daumier, by Nadar. *Courtesy Archives Photographiques, Paris*

his secret self—works that can only be discovered with long and patient search.

All in all, *Rue Transnonain*, *The Republic*, *Ratapoil* will remain eternal. But they are messages in clear language, parts of a dialogue between the artist and the public.

A few other works show us Daumier the man—or at least an epic personage like Don Quixote—walking alone with his back to us down a lonely road toward I know not what unworldly goal to which he never stopped aspiring. These works disclose to us the true and secret soul of this great artist—this (I would also say) great solitary.

BIOGRAPHICAL OUTLINE

1808   FEBRUARY 26: Birth of Honoré Daumier in the Place Saint-Martin, Marseilles.

FEBRUARY 29: Baptism.

1816   Honoré and his mother move to Paris, where his father has preceded them.

1819   A tragedy written by Honoré's father is staged at an amateur theater, Rue Chantereine.

1820–21   Honoré works as errand boy for a process server, and then as a clerk in Delaunay's bookshop, Palais Royal.

1822   Becomes protégé of Alexandre Lenoir, an important early influence.

1823   Enters the Académie Suisse. Halting attempts at lithography. Works for Belliard, lithographer and publisher of contemporary portraits.

1824   First political cartoons.

1828   Drawings signed "H. D."

1829   Political weekly *La Silhouette* is founded; it publishes Daumier's satirical treatments of Charles X and leading politicians.

1830   The July Revolution. Daumier may have taken part in the street fighting. It is believed that he received head wounds. He begins to practice sculpture under influence of the sculptor Préault.

1831   Daumier and his parents are living at 33 Rue de la Barillerie. Aubert and Charles Philipon commission him to do a series of little statues of contemporary political figures.

DECEMBER 15: Publication of the lithograph *Gargantua*.

1832   Daumier and his parents are living at 12 Quai de l'Hôtel de Ville.

FEBRUARY 23: Sentenced by the *Cour d'Assises* to six months in prison and fined 500 francs for "inciting to hatred and contempt of the government and insulting the king." Sentence suspended.

AUGUST 23: He publishes the lithograph *La Cour du Roi Pétaud*.

AUGUST 31: Arrested and sent to the prison of Sainte-Pélagie.

NOVEMBER 11: Transferred to Dr. Pinel's clinic for mental patients.

1833   FEBRUARY: Daumier is released and takes an apartment in the Rue Saint-Denis. Forms close friendships with the painters Narcisse Virgile Diaz, Philippe Auguste Jeanron, Paul Huet, and Gabriel Alexandre Decamps. Spends long hours in The Louvre.

1834   *Rue Transnonain, April 15, 1834* (lithograph).

1835   New laws limiting freedom of the press compel Daumier to abandon political cartoons. Turns to other satirical subjects.

1835–45   Produces a large number of lithographs and has scarcely any time to paint. Is living on the Ile de la Cité (Rue de l'Hirondelle).

1845   Moves to 9 Quai d'Anjou, Ile Saint-Louis.

1846   FEBRUARY 2: Birth of an illegitimate son, recorded under the name of Honoré Daumier.

APRIL 16: Marries Alexandrine Dassy, seamstress.

1846–48   Frequents the painter Boissard de Boisdenier, who lives in the Hôtel Lauzun, where he meets prominent artists and writers, among them Baudelaire. Produces large number of lithographs.

1848   February Revolution; Louis Philippe dethroned. Daumier paints his allegorical study, *The Republic*. Receives commissions from the government.

1849–50 Paintings, sculptures, numerous lithographs.

1851 Louis Napoleon overthrows the republic and becomes Emperor Napoleon III. Daumier's sculpture *Ratapoil*.

1852 Slight changes in his lithographic technique. Baudelaire, Champfleury, and Théodore de Banville publish essays in which Daumier is highly praised.

1853–57 Daumier spends summers at Valmondois. Often visits Barbizon, where he meets Corot, Théodore Rousseau, and Millet.

1858 Illness. Daumier wants to devote himself exclusively to painting and sculpture.

1860 MARCH: *Le Charivari* informs him that it will no longer take his lithographs.

1860–62 Years of joyless work and discouragement.

1863 Daumier moves from the Ile Saint-Louis to Montmartre, where his successive addresses are Boulevard Rochechouart, 26 Rue de l'Abbaye (the present Rue des Abbesses), and 36 Boulevard de Clichy. Spends his summers at Valmondois.

1864 *Le Charivari* offers him a new contract. He continues producing humorous lithographs for a living.

1865 Spends part of the summer at Théodore Rousseau's. Rents a small house at Valmondois.

1867 Daumier meets Gambetta. Begins work on his *Don Quixote*. Threatened with blindness.

1868 Death of Théodore Rousseau and of Baudelaire. Daumier is almost destitute. Corot buys the house in Valmondois where Daumier has been living and gives it to him as a surprise gift.

1877 Daumier is almost blind. The government grants him an annual pension of 2,400 francs.

1878 Big Daumier exhibition at the gallery of Durand-Ruel. Favorable notice. Daumier undergoes two eye operations. His pension is increased to 4,800 francs.

1879 FEBRUARY 11: Death of Daumier.
     APRIL 16: His remains transferred to Père Lachaise cemetery.

SCULPTURE, DRAWINGS, AND WATERCOLORS

52. SELF–PORTRAIT. 1853.
Bronze height 28³/₈″.
Bibliothèque Nationale, Paris

53. RATAPOIL. 1850.
Bronze, height 17$\frac{1}{4}$".
The National Gallery of Art,
Washington, D.C.
Rosenwald Collection, 1951

54. THE BURDEN. 1849–50. Terra cotta, height 13³/₈″. *The Walters Art Gallery, Baltimore*

55. M. GUIZOT
(L'ENNUYEUX). C. 1832.
Bronze, height 8⅝″.
Galerie Sagot-Le Garrec, Paris

56. M. BAILLIOT
(L'INFATUÉ DE SOI). C. 1832.
Bronze, height 7⅛″.
Galerie Sagot-Le Garrec, Paris

57. M. HARLE (LE GATEUX). C. 1832.
Bronze, height 5″.
Collection Joseph H. Hirshhorn,
New York

58. COUNT DE KERATRY
(L'OBSÉQUIEUX).
c. 1832. Bronze, height 5″.
Galerie Sagot–Le Garrec, Paris

59. M. DELORT (LE MOQUER). C. 1832. Bronze, height 9″.
The National Gallery of Art, Washington, D.C.

60. M. PATAILLE (LE GOURMET).
c. 1832. Bronze, height 6³/₄″.
The National Gallery of Art,
Washington, D.C.

61. M. LEFEBVRE
(L'ESPRIT FIN ET TRANCHANT).
Bronze, height 7⁷/₈″.
Collection Joseph H. Hirshhorn,
New York

62. THE BOURGEOIS STROLLER.
Terra cotta, height 7³/₄″.
Private collection, Paris

63. SMALL-FRY LANDLORD.
Bronze, height 7″.
Collection Joseph H. Hirshhorn,
New York

64. EMIGRANTS (first version). 1848–49.
Plaster, 11 × 26″. *The Louvre, Paris*

65. EMIGRANTS. 1848–49. Bronze, 14¹⁄₈ × 29¹⁄₂″.
The National Gallery of Art, Washington, D.C.

66. PRISONERS. C. 1840. Black crayon with wash, $5^1/_4 \times 9^1/_2$".
Bibliothèque, École des Beaux Arts, Paris

67. TWO MEN LOOKING TOWARD THE LEFT. C. 1840.
Pen and pencil, charcoal, sepia wash, $5^7/_8 \times 7^3/_8''$.
The Louvre, Paris

68. THE CONCILIATING JUDGE.
c. 1848. Pen and pale green wash,
$4^3/_4 \times 3^5/_8$". *Private collection, Paris*

69. BEGGARS. C. 1850.
Drawing with wash, $7^1/_2 \times 5^1/_2$".
Boymans–Van Beuningen Museum,
Rotterdam

70. HORSEMAN. Pen and ink, $8\frac{1}{4} \times 10\frac{1}{2}''$.
Collection Claude Roger-Marx, Paris

71. STUDY FOR "THE DONKEY AND THE TWO THIEVES."
c. 1850. Charcoal drawing, 13 × 9¹/₂". Collection Claude Roger-Marx, Paris

72. PLOWING. C. 1850.
Watercolor with India ink wash, $7^1/_8 \times 10^5/_8$".
Private collection, Paris

73. SOUP. c. 1860–62. Pen and wash, 11 × 15³/₄″.
The Louvre, Paris

74. THE THIRD-CLASS CARRIAGE. C. 1862.
Pen and ink wash over charcoal, $9^3/_8 \times 13^1/_8$".
Collection Mr. and Mrs. Norton Simon, Fullerton, California

75. CLOWN. C. 1868. Black chalk and watercolor, 14³/₈ × 10″. *The Metropolitan Museum of Art, New York*

76. MOUNTEBANKS. C. 1855. Gouache and watercolor,
5¼ × 5⅝″. *Private collection, Paris*

77. CONNOISSEURS. c. 1858. Drawing with charcoal and watercolor wash, $9^3/_4 \times 7^1/_8''$.
The Cleveland Museum of Art. Dudley P. Allen Collection

78. THE GOOD FRIENDS. C. 1864.
Pencil, crayon, and watercolor, $9^1/_4 \times 11^7/_8$″.
George A. Lucas Collection, Maryland Institute, Baltimore.
Courtesy The Baltimore Museum of Art

COLORPLATES

Painted about 1843–46

LAWYER READING A DOCUMENT
(*L'Avocat Lisant*)

Oil on canvas, 16³/₈ × 13"

Collection Dr. Robert Bühler, Winterthur, Switzerland

Between 1845 and 1848, Daumier executed a series of lithographs on the theme "Officers of the Law." Daumier did not much care for these people. He is tolerant of judges, whom he most often depicts dozing in their seats; in a few works, *In Camera* for instance, he shows them as patient, a bit world-weary, rather benevolent. Lawyers, however, are among his pet aversions. Daumier saw them as men paid to simulate emotion and pious devotion to justice, but actually smug and insensitive. They arouse an antipathy in him that goes beyond mere caricature. They figure often in his paintings. Moreover, from the plastic point of view the lawyer appealed to Daumier's sculptural genius; he knows so well how to make us feel the presence of the body under the ample drapery of the lawyer's gown. And the motions of the body are often more revealing than the face itself. Daumier brings to mind Ingres (who came, furtively, to look at Daumier's drawings in *Le Charivari*'s window). Ingres also turned drapery to good account, particularly the ample folds of monks' cowls.

The canvas reproduced here is painted with astonishing speed and *brio*. The gown, in the black of which there is a play of very intricate cold tones, stands out powerfully against the yellow background of a corridor in the Palais de Justice. Two blobs of color—the hands (the left one in a curious penumbra)—hold a brief or summons. A few dark touches and one large lighted area (forehead and right cheek) were sufficient for Daumier not only to render the man's professional mask sculpturally, but also to suggest a certain bewilderment in his expression.

Painted about 1843–46

THREE LAWYERS IN CONVERSATION
(*Trois Avocats Causant*)

Oil on canvas, 16 × 13"

Lower left corner: h. Daumier

The Phillips Collection, Washington, D. C.

We have seen that while still a boy employed by a process server, Daumier observed the world of legal chicanery at close quarters. In his home he saw his father, a poet and a man of no very orderly habits, pursued by creditors, trying to put them off with token payments, sometimes as little as three francs. Daumier was reared in an atmosphere of financial worry and lack of thought for the future which he never really outgrew. The account book which has come down to us shows that he almost always earned enough to live comfortably, and we know that his popularity was sufficient to have made his future secure. For instance, in August, 1839, he took in 780 francs, and in September 600 francs—large sums for the period. And yet in 1841 and 1842 a certain Braconneau to whom he owed the sum of 110 francs, "value received in goods" (this suggests a usurer), sued him through a bailiff, one Maître Fumet. Threatened with seizure of his belongings, Daumier tried to gain time; he paid 50 francs, and asked for a postponement. And on April 13, 1842, the court ordered the sale of his furniture! This was the pattern all through his life. In 1862 he borrowed 500 francs from Théodore Rousseau. On another occasion, the photographer Carjat, in answer to his appeal for help, sent him "three louis, all I can afford." On August 10, 1871, Daubigny lent him 500 francs, and on September 29 an additional 250 francs. In 1878, when his faithful friend Geoffroy Dechaume launched his project for a big exhibition at Durand-Ruel's, it was not just to pay tribute to Daumier's work (the artist was seventy), but also to help the aged genius, who was in dire financial straits.

Daumier must often have been summoned to the Palais de Justice by his creditors, but in his works he usually spared bailiffs, law clerks, and the other small fry of the bar. What caught his eye repeatedly was the lawyers he saw rushing up and down the corridors, their black gowns flapping, forever busy and exuding a sense of their own importance. The law provided him with motifs of which he never tired. He exploited this particular milieu frequently between 1830 and 1860.

Painted about 1843–48

THE MOONLIGHT WALK *(Les Noctambules)*

Oil on panel, 11 × 7³/₈″

National Museum of Wales, Cardiff

This very curious night scene shows two men standing bemused along the river, looking at the houses opposite. A full moon bathes the scene in a diffuse light. Daumier must often have sensed the mystery of the sleeping city, a mystery which also affected Balzac. He moved to 9 Quai d'Anjou about 1845; his lodging was modest, but with it went a big attic that he could use as a studio. He had a spiral staircase built for easy access. The landlord several times hinted that he should pay a little more rent since he was using the attic, but the artist, who was always short of money, managed never to take the hint. His studio was very unlike the studios of fashionable artists as contemporary novelists depicted them: a clutter of precious fabrics, medieval weapons, every sort of romantic bric-à-brac. All Daumier kept there was the tools of his trade, drawing pencils, lithographic stones, portfolios crammed with drawings, and lumps of modeling clay. The walls were bare save for two lithographs by Delacroix, a landscape, and a lithograph by Nanteuil of *The Pariahs*, a plaster group by Préault which had been rejected by the Salon of 1835. There were also a few medallions by David d'Angers, whose opinions were very leftist, like Daumier's.

From this studio he had a fine view. On the one side he could see a little arm of the Seine lined with *bateaux-lavoirs* and places where horses were watered. On the other side the towers of Notre Dame loomed majestically in the distance, and he could see the domes of La Salpetrière and the Val-de-Grâce, as well as that of the Panthéon. From this observation point up under the rooftops he must often have looked out over the sleeping city in the quiet of the night, just as the two figures in this painting are doing.

Painted about 1845

A CORNER IN THE PALAIS DE JUSTICE
(Un Coin du Palais)

Oil on canvas, 13 × 9⁷/₈″

Lower left corner: h. Daumier

Musée des Beaux-Arts, Lyons

This composition, long known as *The Two Lawyers*, was repeated by Daumier in his *Lawyers Leaving the Palais*. The painting belonged at one time to the landscape painter Charles François Daubigny, a friend of Daumier's. There is an air of almost priestly solemnity in the affected manner of the principal figure. Daumier has eagerly turned to account here the plastic elements he finds in lawyers' gowns and attitudes. However, he has only contempt for their false emotions and theatrical gestures. There is a drawing by him, inspired by Proudhon's famous painting, *La Justice et la Vengeance Poursuivant le Crime (Justice and Revenge Pursuing Crime)*, in which the criminal being pursued is a lawyer.

In the work reproduced here, the self-important lawyer stands in front of a great pilaster with quadruple fluting whose dimensions suggest how high the column must be. The background is swallowed up in dignified shadow. We are indeed within a temple. As for the other lawyer, whom the first passes without deigning to notice, Daumier gives scant attention to his features, so as to impress upon us his insignificance in relation to the legal lion. The latter's features, on the other hand, are powerfully and sculpturally rendered. The respectful attitude and shy glance with which the poor lawyer turns toward his illustrious colleague, who steps out vigorously so that his gown flows out behind him, makes this both an admirable piece of painting and a fleeting but intense bit of psychological drama. No one interprets blacks better than Daumier. The more his blacks fall in a zone of shadow, the more richly and variously are they composed and modulated.

Painted 1848

THE REPUBLIC *(La République)*

Oil on canvas, 29¹/₂ × 23⁵/₈"
The Louvre, Paris

Louis Philippe was overthrown on February 25, 1848, and the provisional government of the Republic was formed. Daumier saw in these events the triumph of his political ideal—a pure, lofty ideal, which he was to express in this unforgettable manner. The new regime required a suitable symbolic image, and artists were invited to compete to supply it. On April 27 more than 100 unsigned sketches were exhibited at the École des Beaux-Arts.

The jury was composed of Lamartine, Delacroix, Ingres, Decamps, Delaroche, Meissonnier, Thoré, and Jeanron. Twenty sketches were approved, including one by Daumier, which was superior to all the others. Courbet, not usually shy about his own genius, refused to enter the competition so that Daumier might win. The twenty artists were asked to expand their sketches into large-scale designs.

Daumier was always the least punctual of men. Despite his friends' urging he kept putting off the task. As time went by, the political situation changed. Within three months of the February Revolution the conservative parties had gained in influence, and the bloody repressions of June were the result. In the end, Daumier's *Republic* was never enlarged from this first sketch.

Never has that particular political entity, the Republic, been paid more impressive artistic tribute. Daumier saw the Republic as a kind of nourishing divinity, a strong, healthy female at once fertile and chaste. Modeled in large planes, its monumental character owes much to powerful contrasts of lighting. Should we be sorry that Daumier never expanded this sketch? Could he have preserved its august quality in a painting of heroic size?

74

Painted about 1848–49

REFUGEES *(Les Fugitifs)*

Oil on wood, 6 × 11⁷/₈″

Lower left corner: h. Daumier

Collection Mrs. William Van Horne, Montreal

In this treatment of the theme of flight, the movement of the refugees is from left to right, and away from the viewer. In other respects as well, the work differs from *The Emigrants* (following plate). Here he has blurred outlines and subdued his colors. The group is less compact than in the other painting, as though enveloped in some sort of mist. The human figures, the horses, even the dog, all have their heads down and are treated only as volumes. Some imminent disaster is driving these runaways on, and the desolation of the landscape helps create a mood no less poignant and mysterious than the rather larger painting on this theme in Winterthur, Switzerland.

In another painting formerly in the Durand-Ruel collection, Daumier also depicted people in flight. They are seen at the edge of a forest. In a painting formerly in the Haller collection, he depicts winded horses. Finally, he gave full rein to his sculptural genius in an admirable, overpowering bas-relief entitled *The Emigrants*, for which he made several drawings. Works like this bas-relief and *Ratapoil* lead one to the conclusion that Daumier was one of the three geniuses of "movement" in nineteenth-century French sculpture, along with Degas and Rodin. It is noteworthy that two of them are still best known as painters and draftsmen.

Daumier made two slightly differing versions of his bas-relief, which he left in the original clay. Geoffroy Dechaume had plaster casts made of these before they crumbled away. The original plaster of the first variant (fig. 64) was recently acquired by the Louvre. In it, the emigrants are rushing headlong, as though pushed by some centrifugal force toward some improbable promised land. The powerful males carry the newborn, while the children who can walk urge their elders on, tugging at their hands. The ample, robust females hurry on with a certain sadness, as though recalling the members of the tribe it has been necessary to leave to die by the wayside, unable to keep up.

Painted about 1848–49

EMIGRANTS *(Les Émigrants)*

Oil on canvas, 15 × 26³/₈″

Lower right corner: h. Daumier

Collection Oscar Reinhart, Winterthur, Switzerland

The more closely we study Daumier today, the more he seems to us different from the Daumier his contemporaries knew and appreciated: the cartoonist, the observer of his age's foibles, of the worthy man who would rather shrug than contradict anyone or get involved in a discussion. And yet there were two Daumiers from the first. Besides the one whose friends thought he had no secrets, there was a Daumier who reveals himself only in works like this one, where some obsession with flight is expressed with magnificent pictorial means.

This painting has long been known as *Emigrants*, but to us it expresses more than a mere search for a new home: this is a whole people on the move, an exodus, the drama of all "displaced persons" everywhere. Their poor rags whipped by a cold wind, these people are driven away from somewhere. Their progress through a mountainous country without roads is painful, yet they force themselves forward. Who are they? Where are they coming from? It is impossible to say. All but naked, there is no detail about them that ties them to a particular time and place. This is mankind itself on the run. Could this work be related to Decamps' *Defeat of the Cimbri*, which aroused a considerable amount of praise when it was painted? I do not think so. Could it be alluding to the deportations after the counterrevolutionary events of June, 1848? Again, I do not think so. Daumier treated this theme so often that I believe it reflects some personal obsession.

The painting is of great pictorial richness; bright reds, blues, chrome yellows, blue-greens, and lakes blaze up here and there. The soil, the hills, the sinister sky are splendidly rendered.

This little picture is great painting.

78

Painted about 1849

THE MILLER, HIS SON, AND THE DONKEY
(Le Meunier, son Fils et l'Ane)

Oil on canvas, 51¹/₈ × 38¹/₄"

Lower right corner: h. Daumier

Corporation of Glasgow. Burrell Collection

Daumier did not paint many large pictures. However, when attacking certain subjects, he felt the need to give fairly broad scope to his gifts as a colorist. Having made a thorough study of Rubens and the great French painters of the seventeenth century, and feeling himself capable of resurrecting the richness and iridescence of their pigments, he did in a few cases make use of vast formats.

As in *The Donkey and the Two Thieves* (page 107), Daumier here took his subject from La Fontaine's *Fables*. Is there some political intention in this picture? If so, it is very subtle. The unhappy trio of the miller, his son, and the donkey did not interest Daumier much; these are scarcely dealt with at all, being relegated to the background, although the outlines of the two men are sufficiently expressive to suggest that they feel at a loss, unable as they are to please everybody. What did interest Daumier was the group of three sturdy, laughing young women, bursting with Rubens-like vitality. They are walking toward us, and their lively motions are communicated to the materials of their costumes—as much draperies as clothing. The pigment is sumptuous; all the parts situated in shadow have a marvelously nuanced half-light. The right arm of the girl at the left is a model of coloring in full chiaroscuro, and the still life of the fruit she carries must have enchanted Courbet.

Painted about 1849–50

THE DRUNKENNESS OF SILENUS
(La Marche de Silène)

Drawing with gouache, $18^7/_8 \times 24^5/_8$"

Lower left: h. Daumier

Musée des Beaux-Arts, Calais

Although not a painting in the strict sense, this drawing has been so abundantly touched up with gouache that it can be classified among Daumier's painted works. It was inspired by an engraving of a work by Rubens.

Daumier used certain elements of this composition in several other works. The obese Silenus, most notably, resembles one of his favorite figures of caricature—Véron, a physician who was director of the Opéra (and became rich in this post), founder of the *Revue de Paris*, and lastly editor of *Constitutionnel*, the most extreme pro-government newspaper under the Second Empire.

Daumier must have been fond of this theme, the reluctant march of Silenus, for he treated it again with variants under the title *Le Cortège de Silène (The Procession of Silenus)*. The Goncourts, though they were not very familiar with Daumier's work, were the first to call attention to this picture, and to speak of him as a painter.

The gouache drawing reproduced here was exhibited at the Salon of 1850. We have elsewhere noted that on September 19, 1848, Jeanron (then in charge of the state museums) had forwarded to Daumier a letter from Charles Blanc, head of the Académie des Beaux-Arts, informing the artist that the Ministry of the Interior was commissioning him to execute a painting for 1,000 francs, and asking him to submit a sketch for approval. The letter was addressed to "Citizen Daumier," and it closed with "*Salut et Fraternité*" ("Fraternal Greetings"). Despite the savage way the street fighting of June had been put down, revolutionary etiquette was still being observed. Five months later, on February 10, 1849, the Republic had become more respectable. On that date Charles Blanc addressed a letter to *Monsieur* Daumier, *peintre*, which notified him that the fee for his commission had been raised to 1,500 francs.

The unreliable Daumier never executed this commission. Time after time, M. du Bois, an inspector for the Beaux-Arts, called on the painter to find out how the work was progressing, but to no avail. Not until fourteen years later, in 1863, did Daumier suggest settling the matter by giving the government this *March of Silenus*, which had been in his studio since 1850. Following an unenthusiastic report by M. de Bois, the offer was accepted, on condition that the painting be delivered framed. It was assigned to the museum in Calais. Several years later, Arago, head of the Beaux-Arts, granted the aged, half-blind artist, who was in financial distress, a pension of 2,400 francs a year. He asked that the *Silenus* be hung in his office. But the work was already in Calais and has remained there.

Painted about 1849–50

NYMPHS PURSUED BY SATYRS
(Nymphes Poursuivies par des Satyres)

Oil on canvas, 51⁵/₈ × 38¹/₄"

Lower right corner: h. D.

Montreal Museum of Fine Arts. Miss Adaline Van Horne Bequest, 1945

This painting was exhibited at the Salon of 1850, where only a few critics noticed it. Claude Vignon praised it, and Clément de Ris was even more enthusiastic; M. de Chennevière, on the other hand, spoke of it with great severity as a work at best suitable for decorating a cabaret, and much inferior to Daumier's least important lithographs. At the end of his review he spoke in favorable terms of a painting by Gavarni, contrasting it with Daumier's.

The episode indicates to what extent Daumier's fame as a lithographer hurt him when he exhibited his paintings. Other artists, however, were all aware that he was a painter; one contemporary cartoon represents him with a palette and brushes. But to the public at large he was a lithographer, and a lithographer he was expected to remain. M. de Chennevière's review also exemplifies a contemporary tendency to set Gavarni against Daumier—a tendency that eventually gave rise to an unfounded legend to the effect that the two were personal enemies. The painting reproduced here obliges us to insist on the influence of Lenoir's teaching on Daumier. Lenoir was nearly sixty when the young Daumier became his pupil. Daumier's father, the poet from Marseilles, became a close friend of Lenoir, and one of Daumier's sisters mended the famous archaeologist's shirts. Lenoir had studied under Van Loo and Doyen. During the revolution he had rescued and collected a number of beautiful vestiges of medieval and Renaissance architecture, which he gave to the famous museum of the Grand Augustins in Paris (today the École des Beaux-Arts). He taught Daumier to love and admire not only the ancients, but also Titian, Rubens, Fragonard, etc. Incidentally, Daumier made a copy (since destroyed) of Rubens' *Kermesse*. Rubens is very much present in the painting shown here. The panic flight of the nymphs sets their draperies to fluttering wildly. Flashes of yellow furrow the skirt, and the flesh tones are abundantly splashed with sunlight. There is not a single flat tone, all are modeled and vibrant. It is hard to understand the almost total indifference of the public of 1850 to such a work.

Painted about 1850

"WE WANT BARABBAS"
(*"Nous Voulons Barabbas"*)

Grisaille on canvas, 63 × 50"

Folkwang Museum, Essen

An ardent republican throughout the reign of Napoleon III, Daumier managed to avoid catching so much as a glimpse of the emperor and his retinue, even in the street. He was also anticlerical. Enthusiastic at the revolution which ushered in the republic in February, 1848, he was inspired to begin the magnificent unfinished painting now in the Louvre *(The Republic, page 75).* No sooner had the new regime come to power, however, than the left unleashed a mass movement which terrified the middle classes. As early as June the new government was savagely repressing it. The regime continued to call itself a republic, though the party dissensions which were shortly to bring about its downfall were already dividing the new state. As it became more and more "conservative," the republic showed itself more and more friendly to the clergy.

Republicans who had joined the regime at the beginning, men like Jeanron and Charles Blanc, kept their posts. Thanks to them Daumier was given commissions, probably for religious pictures. Such commissions may account for some of Daumier's unfinished works, like this one. This project, of exceptionally large format, is executed in grisaille. The figures are drawn with very thick lines. The work is comparable to a somewhat smaller sketch in the Rijksmuseum in Amsterdam, which represents Jesus and the disciples as humble folk. It is not impossible that Daumier took pleasure in opposing to the "bourgeois" conception of Christ his own conception, depicting him as the gentle tribune, consoler of the eternally exploited, the Christ who had been called the "*sans-culotte Jésus*" under the French Revolution.

Another religious subject treated by Daumier is his *The Repentant Magdalen*. In this case we are more certain that it was a government commission, for it remained in the possession of M. François Cavé, a department head at the Beaux-Arts. Daumier probably submitted it as a sketch and then never took it back to finish—a typical example of his carelessness about commissions. Very different in treatment from this Barabbas, *The Repentant Magdalen* is a powerful Rubens-like nude, modeled in a very full gamut of browns.

86

Painted about 1850–58

RETURN FROM MARKET *(Le Retour du Marché)*

Oil on canvas, $14^5/_8 \times 11^1/_2"$

Collection Oscar Reinhart, Winterthur, Switzerland

This painting is somewhat exceptional among Daumier's works. He had no sympathy for what he saw of Impressionism in its earliest days. And yet like Daubigny, with whom he had so much in common, Daumier was a precursor of Impressionism, for all that he never suspected it. In the canvas reproduced here, he is primarily concerned with the diffuse light that bathes the outlines and blurs the volumes to the point where they are nearly obliterated. The head and upper body of the peasant woman sitting on top of the saddlebags are scarcely modeled, and the ground has been rendered with fast, glissando brush strokes.

Daumier was here very much on the path that was to lead the Impressionists to give ever more importance to changes of light and air, ever less to the solidity of forms. This painting amazes us; in it, Daumier is far from his usual self. Undoubtedly, the donkey's head and ears provided the artist with a motif for pretty color modulations. The animal's legs are indicated in very dark outline, such as is to be found in many of Daumier's works. But the peasant woman's hand has been drawn cursorily. The fact of the matter is that Daumier lacked the soul of the peasant. The life of the fields, the endless toil of rural existence, did not much inspire him. He never had the opportunity to become really acquainted with it, still less to participate in it. How little feeling he had on this score becomes clear when we single out from his countless lithographs a number devoted to some petty bourgeois (as little suited to physical labor as himself) who has retired to the country and stands in front of his little villa, beaming with joy at the one scrawny leafless tree in his grassless yard.

Painted about 1850

WOMEN AND CHILDREN UNDER A TREE
(Femmes et Enfants sous un Arbre)

Oil on wood, 12⅝ × 7⅛"

Lower left corner: h. D.

Rijksmuseum H. W. Mesdag, The Hague

By his trade, his friends, and his tastes Daumier was very much a city dweller. He often made fun of the middle-class dream of a little house in the suburbs with its own garden. Nonetheless Daumier had real feeling for open spaces running off into the distance. One of his 1848 lithographs stands with the finest treatments ever made of landscape in the rain. The lithograph shows a man of petty bourgeois background under an umbrella, wearing a top hat and fishing in the rain. His wife, in shawl and bonnet, is asking: "Aren't we ever going home?" We are made to feel that what had begun as a shower has turned into a steady downpour. The banks of the stream are bare. One little tree, quite far back in the composition, is bending under the rain. The sky is darkly overcast as far as the eye can see. The man seems unaware of the desolation around him, he keeps on fishing. The much more famous *Poor Fisherman* by Puvis de Chavannes does not begin to convey the poignancy of this subject as well as Daumier's painting does.

Daumier is most susceptible to the charms of nature and the countryside when he introduces human figures into such compositions. It is through them that such scenes come alive for him. He scarcely notices children, except when they are at one, so to speak, with their mothers—as in the group shown here, captured in all its simplicity. His only "property" is the tree under which the two peasant women stand talking. The right arm of the woman holding the sleeping child over her hip is drawn with marvelous flexibility and truth. The child standing in the foreground brings to mind the splendid ragamuffin in Courbet's big *Studio*.

Daumier had many friends among the group of painters who worked at Barbizon, near the Fontainebleau forest. One of their most enthusiastic collectors was the Dutch painter Hendrick Willem Mesdag, and the painting reproduced here was in his collection. He bequeathed it to the city of The Hague in 1903.

90

Painted about 1852

AFTER SCHOOL *(La Sortie de l'École)*

Oil on panel, 15³/₄ × 12¹/₄″

Lower left corner: h. Daumier

Collection Alfred Daber, Paris

This painting embodies a type of composition unusual in Daumier's work. As we have repeatedly observed, Daumier found the subject of childhood congenial only in scenes of mothers and children. We sometimes get the impression that he was unhappy about this and tried to force an interest in childhood. Actually, however, only the very young moved him, babes in arms, or the little boy in one of the paintings depicting traveling circus performers, whom poverty has turned into a little old man.

In the work shown here, the figures are not, properly speaking, children, but nearly mature girls and women. What must have attracted him in this scene of pent-up energies set free is the play of color: the blue of a work jacket, the yellow of a scarf, the red of a hooded cape, with the whites of the linen punctuating the chromatic hodgepodge.

One inspiration for this lively scene may have been Décamps' *Turkish Children,* a scene of happy young people leaving the mosque after religious instruction. Exhibited at the Salon of 1842, the work was widely admired. Our surmise is the more plausible because Décamps and Daumier often treated the same themes, *Don Quixote* for example, and La Fontaine's fable, "The Donkey and the Two Thieves."

Painted about 1852

THE BATHERS *(Avant le Bain)*

Oil on canvas, $9^7/_8 \times 12^3/_8$"

Corporation of Glasgow. Burrell Collection

In this canvas Daumier aimed at an effect of back lighting. In the lighter portions, in his way of treating water and sky, of enveloping in air, so to speak, the boy walking down to the stream, we detect the quality that has often caused him to be regarded as a precursor of the Impressionists. At the same time, however, while effects of light and air interest him and hold his attention, he treats the tree and its foliage as elements of a flat *décor*. In this he differs radically from his good friend Corot, who always rendered trees and bushes in terms of volume.

Particularly noteworthy in this connection is the fact that artists whose careers were just getting under way when Daumier's was ending were obviously influenced by his works of this type. I refer especially to Seurat.

From 1882 on, Seurat composed a number of studies for a painting on the theme of *Une Baignade à Asnières*, now in the Tate Gallery, London. It was rejected by the official Salon of 1884 and was exhibited at the first Salon des Indépendants that same year. His studies incorporate everything we see here, even the gesture of the boy who is taking off his shirt. Could this be a mere coincidence? I do not think so.

At all events, we may say that in works such as this one Daumier anticipated Seurat's "divisionism," which was eventually codified into a systematic doctrine but which, based as it is on the law of contrasts, is present in all great works of all ages.

The treatment of the tree branches against the sky is an unusually violent exploitation of contrasting tones.

Painted about 1852–56

LITTLE PEASANT GIRLS *(Les Petites Paysannes)*

Oil on wood, 11³/₈ × 7⁷/₈″

Collection Dr. Warner Muensterberger, New York

In his lithographs and cartoons Daumier displays indifference to children. Indeed, his aversion for middle-class society often extends to its offspring. In his paintings, however, he displays more tenderness, and we find several figures of children captured with great sensitivity. In no medium, however, does his vision of the child have anything in common with—for example—that of English painters. Daumier sees the child as a little animal, whose awkwardness is rather amusing, as a puppy's is. It is his candor in setting down just what he sees—a candor remote from all "literary" attitudes—that creates the charm of works such as the one reproduced here, quite apart from admirable pictorial qualities and luminosity. It is noteworthy that the two children in this painting, the very young one and the slightly older sister who is already taking care of the baby, are unmistakably *peasant* children. We are reminded of an artist with whom Daumier had profound affinities, himself a rustic, who was dogged by bad luck, and who very often painted peasants and peasant children. This was Millet, who lived for the most part at Barbizon, on the edge of the Fontainebleau forest. Daumier and Millet certainly influenced each other in matters of technique, and possibly also with respect to subjects treated.

In October, 1865, Daumier went to the village of Auvers near Pontoise. It seems evident that works of this type, which so effectively render country life, must have been painted in the region of Auvers.

Painted about 1854–56

MEMBERS OF THE BAR *(Membres du Barreau)*

Oil on wood, 8³/₄ × 11″

Lower left corner: h. D.

Collection Mr. and Mrs. Charles Goldman, New York

Daumier had personal experience with the minor workings of the law, especially with bailiffs. Balzac told him one day that in order to be a genius, one should "get into debt." Daumier was only too inclined to follow this advice. However, the lawsuits he was involved in were never important enough to be handled by these lords of the Palais de Justice, the great lawyers. Yet these men held great fascination for Daumier, a profound psychologist in addition to being a painter and a sculptor. The broad folds of the lawyers' gowns with their loose sleeves appealed to the sculptor in him, providing ample mobile volumes, which he enjoyed modeling. The painter in Daumier enjoyed endowing these figures with intense life and significance by means of the movements and postures he impressed upon them. Here, he shows them almost like members of a crowd, this particular group dominated by the corpulent figure in the foreground, whose glance is impressively devoid of any expression whatever. The others in the group seem to be stirring within a half-light suggestive of some sacred temple, whose majesty they are trying to reflect.

At the Daumier exhibition in 1878, Gambetta (one of the great lawyers of the day) was greatly impressed when he discovered and could name one after another the legal leading lights of France in Daumier's pictures. He was astonished when Geoffroy Dechaume told him that actually Daumier had never known any of them, for he had not been near the Palais for more than ten years. Like Molière, Daumier created a human type—the lawyer—more eternally true than any actual individual.

Painted about 1854–56

DON QUIXOTE AND SANCHO PANZA

Oil on canvas, 26 × 45⁵/₈"

Private collection, Zurich

This study is one of the most astonishing of several works inspired by Cervantes' novel, no doubt a sketch for a large painting never made. We might almost be glad of it, for this unfinished canvas gives us a chance to study Daumier's habit of first working out everything in planes and in terms of contrasts between light and shadow. By such sober, powerful means he worked out much more than merely the volumes. There is mastery here, utter sureness as to just what is to be expressed. By these purely plastic procedures, we have already the very souls of the characters. Sancho is a squat, heavy figure on a donkey that plods along docilely; the man's belly and right leg are in almost opaque shadow. Don Quixote riding ahead is as different as he can be: a crystalline ghost made up entirely of angles, astride his absurd Rosinante. Caught up wholly in his dream, he is weightless—the outline is not really of a human body. He is the pellucid spirit of the heroic obsession that animates him as he makes his way through the lunar landscape. This is very different from frivolous, anecdotal conceptions of Cervantes' hero (Charles Antoine Coypel's seventeenth-century compositions, for example).

In 1836 an edition of *Don Quixote* appeared with 800 engraved vignettes after Tony Johannot. Gustave Doré's illustrations appeared in 1863. Remarkable as both these works are, neither achieves the tragic grandeur of Daumier's *Don Quixote*.

Painted about 1855–60

THE BEER DRINKERS *(Les Buveurs de Bière)*

Oil on wood, $8^7/_8 \times 10^5/_8''$

Lower left corner: h. Daumier

Collection Dr. Fritz Nathan, Zurich

There have been frequent mentions of Daumier's fondness for wine—indeed, rather too much has been made of it. However, if he really liked to drink, was it not primarily because he was attracted by the peaceful, relaxed atmosphere of the modest *cafés* he seemed to favor? They were a refuge to him. In one of his short stories, Pierre Mac Orlan uses the expression *"La maison du retour écœurant"* ("Home that it sickens you to go back to"). There may well have been days when Daumier felt that way about his household. To be sure, he was a good husband, but in a rather resigned way. "Didine," his good-natured wife, was poorly educated, and it is unlikely that he found in her the understanding he needed. Besides, as soon as he got back home he was very likely to find an impatient demand from *Le Charivari* for immediate delivery of a drawing, or a messenger sent to fetch a still-unfinished lithographic stone.

From his choice of subjects we can see that although he preferred humble working-class *cafés*, he was also perfectly familiar with more "bourgeois" establishments where the customers did not favor *le gros rouge* and *le bleu* (colloquial terms for the commonest, cheapest red wine), but beer, a beverage regarded as smarter, more respectable.

The setting here seems to be one of these "better" *cafés*. The better tailored clothes, the better groomed faces of the drinkers, the very blondness of the beer they sip, all this is rendered in a fairly bright tonal atmosphere in which all the diverse elements are harmonized.

Painted about 1856

THE DRINKERS *(Les Deux Buveurs)*

Oil on wood, 14⁵/₈ × 11"

Lower left corner: h. D.

The Metropolitan Museum of Art, New York. Bequest of Margaret S. Lewisohn, 1954

This is one of the works in which Daumier's drawing is at its boldest. At the beginning of his career he must have felt a certain fondness for untidy clothing and coarse language—hangovers from his art-student years. When he was imprisoned at Sainte-Pélagie, his fellow inmates called him "Gargantua" (his print of that name adorned many a cell) or "La Gouape"—a slang term denoting someone who is lazy, slovenly, and drinks too much.

Certainly he was not lazy—witness his enormous output. It is by no means sure that he drank too much. We know that he liked to spend time in a little *bistro* on the Ile Saint-Louis (at the corner of the Rue de "la Femme sans Tête" and the Quai Bourbon) with his friends, the bargemen. He must also have joined Baudelaire often at a little *café* hard by the Moulin de Montsouris, at the outskirts of Paris near the Porte d'Orléans. Gavarni reports a visit to his studio, where he found men sitting on the floor around the stove, "each with his own bottle." Daumier was not a snob and probably sometimes offered his hospitality to the homeless of the river front—a breed of down-and-outs notoriously fond of the bottle. All this, and perhaps the fact that he sometimes bragged about his own alcoholic capacity, helped to create the legend (which Cézanne, for example, believed) of a drunkard Daumier. But the man to whom Delacroix wrote on May 16, 1850, "There are few men I respect and admire more than you," could never have been a drunkard.

The two drinkers portrayed here were conceived as an illustration to a passage from Baudelaire's *Vin des Chiffonniers*. (Jean Adhémar tells us that Daumier owned the manuscript of this poem.) Drunkenness has never been expressed more seriously. The figure at the left, who is trying to pull himself together, sticks out his chest and raises his elbow exaggeratedly to pour another drink. His clothes hang loosely on him, indeed, he seems about to lose his jacket. The man at the right is still further along, beginning to sink into an alcoholic stupor. He will fall off the bench in a moment. . . .

Painted about 1856–58

THE DONKEY AND THE TWO THIEVES
(L'Ane et les Deux Voleurs)

Oil on canvas, 23¹/₄ × 14¹/₈"

Lower right corner: h. Daumier

The Louvre, Paris

Daumier almost never dated his works, and since the various periods of his life are not matched by truly different techniques, it is very difficult to date, even approximately, some of his paintings and sculptures. Of course, the situation is not the same in respect to his lithographs, since most of them refer to current events.

Daumier made several versions of *The Donkey and the Two Thieves*. He may have planned to compose a painting on this subject for the Salon of 1860. According to Jean Adhémar, the version reproduced here was painted much later, at a time when Prussia, Austria, and Russia were contending with each other over matters concerning the Near East. Diplomatic rivalries became so fierce that a new partition of Europe seemed imminent.

However, when Daumier refers to international developments, he is usually more direct and explicit than this. Therefore we think that the subject merely gave him an opportunity to show two bodies locked in violent combat. His masterful knowledge of anatomy in action asserts itself in his treatment of the back of the man who temporarily has the upper hand. In the right forearm of the man on the ground we find the same accent as in *Man on a Rope* (page 127). The flesh and the clothing are treated with superb mastery. The whites (e.g., the torn sleeve of the prone figure) are compounded of refined tones. It must be recalled that although Daumier copied old masters and often thought of himself as a follower of Rembrandt, he recalled that Alexandre Lenoir had guided him to appreciate the charm and power of the great eighteenth-century colorists. It is of Fragonard's palette that we are reminded by the bright lights, the Rubens-like flesh, and the sweeping treatment of the ground and the background.

Painted about 1856–60

COUPLE SINGING *(Le Couple Chantant)*

Oil on canvas, 14³/₈ × 11¹/₄″

Lower left corner: h. D.

Rijksmuseum H. W. Mesdag, The Hague

Daumier was not a music lover, and yet several of his works show figures gathered to sing or play music. Occasionally he makes fun of them. For example, a lithograph of 1858 entitled *An Orchestra in a Genteel Household (Un Orchestre dans une Maison Comme il Faut)* is clearly conceived as a caricature. Nor are professional musicians spared his comic verve, as in the lithograph (fig. 23) where he shows a musician in a pit orchestra overcome with yawning (and no draftsman ever painted yawns better than Daumier) while he waits for the dramatic scene on stage to end. That particular lithograph is just one of a whole series.

   This work, however, is not about a boring play or a fashionable musical evening. We have said that if Daumier was ever in love, it could only have been for a very short time, but he was not incapable of tenderness. What he shows in this painting is a young couple unmistakably of modest social background. Their common effort to make out the notes on the score held by the girl and the way their heads come close suggest that they are in love, and happy to be together. And though Daumier is anything but an occultist, he bathes the two in a kind of golden aura, which some would interpret as an emanation of happiness. The woman is painted wholly in this tone, both bust and face. The form is indicated only by a few white highlights near the collarbone and the temple. This is a grave, contemplative work, which discloses a whole private area of Daumier's sensibility.

Painted about 1856–60

THE MELODRAMA *(Le Mélodrame)*

Oil on canvas, 38¹/₄ × 35″

Lower left corner: h. Daumier

Neue Pinakothek, Munich

Daumier was well acquainted with every facet of the theatrical world, with life backstage as well as out front. His father, the glazier-poet whose poems, published at his own expense, had not paid for themselves, went on to try his hand at playwriting. Some time before 1815 he wrote a tragedy entitled *Philip II*. He represented the gloomy king of Spain as jealous of his son Carlos, who had developed a passion for Philip II's wife Elizabeth. Jean Adhémar thinks this play may contain echoes of the author's personal experience, basing this hypothesis on poems by Daumier *père* that suggest he had at some time been loved by a latter-day Phaedra. He succeeded in getting the tragedy produced in 1819 by a modest amateur theater in the Rue Chantereine. It was at best a *succès d'estime*.

Young Honoré was then eleven years old. Endowed with an extraordinary gift for observation, he hung about backstage, attended rehearsals, and watched the actors sometimes from the prompter's booth, sometimes from a cheap seat in the gallery. He was to remember this all his life, and references to the theatrical world turn up often in his works in one form or another.

In this canvas Daumier's intentions are not in the least satirical. He makes great use of the strong contrast between the lighted stage and the dark theater. We cannot help recalling Rembrandt, and must admire Daumier for having succeeded in modeling the spectators in the dark foreground with such variety. These spectators are quite ordinary people. The little light cast from the stage is enough for him to bring out the outlines of the faces and to sculpt them, as it were. At the same time he records their intense, naïvely sincere interest in the action. In this work, where all the elements go so well together, note the marvelous way the actress has been painted, how the intensity of her movement has been captured, and how subtly Daumier has modulated the colors of the stage set.

Painted about 1857–60

THE PRINT COLLECTOR
(L'Amateur d'Estampes)

Oil on canvas, 15³/₄ × 12⁵/₈"

Lower left corner: h. Daumier

Musée du Petit-Palais, Paris

Although Daumier's hand is unmistakable in all his works, his palette varies according to whether he treats a theme borrowed from mythology or fable, as in *Nymphs Pursued by Satyrs* (page 85) and *The Donkey and the Two Thieves* (page 107), or subjects directly observed, as is the case here. The palette is less brilliant, but perhaps all the more nuanced for that. The art lover was one of his favorite subjects between 1855 and 1866.

Daumier lived among collectors of prints and paintings. His friends Daubigny and Millet, among others, were skillful etchers, and he knew well their lithographs and etchings.

Evidently Daumier had a need for solitude which his busy life did not gratify, which seems to be expressed in works like this one, where we see an art lover stopping, in the course of his solitary stroll, in a print dealer's shop. All by himself, he is leafing through portfolios, searching for he knows not what, no doubt some print whose originality or rarity will instantly catch his eye. Just how absorbed he is, how keenly he is looking at the prints, is rendered by the profile in shadow and the position of his body. The pigment here is sumptuous, the whites of the papers in the portfolio are extremely subtly nuanced, and the shadow the collector casts on it is enriched by a play of marvelously combined colder tones. Also note the blue of the portfolio behind the figure, and the way this blue is carried from the half-light to the stream of light that sets it ablaze.

Daumier has left no part of the painting unfinished. There is not one area, not even areas in shadow—as under the counter where the portfolios rest—that is not elaborately nuanced. Here Daumier is the equal even of the greatest master of chiaroscuro, Rembrandt. The light reaches everywhere to give everything depth and form. A painting like this can be looked at for a long time, for ever new riches are to be discovered.

Painted about 1858–60

CRISPIN AND SCAPIN

Oil on canvas, 23⁵/₈ × 32¹/₄"

The Louvre, Paris

Daumier, whose sense of irony was always keen, had great admiration for the genius of Molière. He never said so explicitly, but some of his works, including this one, leave no doubt about it. The artist who made such successful use of Robert Macaire, the nineteenth-century rascal and liar par excellence, must have been deeply impressed by Molière's swindlers and sharpers. Here, the figures (probably Scapin, and Sylvestre disguised as Crispin, the main characters in the *Fourberies de Scapin*) stand in the glare of footlights, so that Daumier can let the light play powerfully on the salient features of their faces, hollowing out the eye sockets and emphasizing in sharp relief the neck muscles of the figure on the right. Scapin wears a white servant's costume, but cold blue tones play over this white, which becomes slightly warmer in those parts of the sleeves that receive the full glare from below. The whites in the facing of Crispin's garment are different in quality, high-keyed and creamy. His cloak and jerkin seem black, but it is a black compounded of infinitely subtle tones. The intricate, skillfully managed play of colors cannot be overemphasized. The most amazing thing of all is that the cunning of the figures, what might be called their state of mind, is expressed less by their facial features than by their movement as a whole. It is not only with his ear that Scapin is attending to Crispin's roguish suggestions, but with his whole left shoulder, his whole body.

Daumier almost never dated his works, but we know that in 1858 he published a very similar composition in *Le Charivari*.

Painted about 1860

CARRYING THE LAUNDRY *(Le Fardeau)*

Oil on canvas, 57⁷/₈ × 37¹/₂"

Lower right corner: h. D.

Collection Ernest Gutzviller, Paris

Daumier rarely discussed his own works, but he prized this exceptionally large canvas.

As we have seen, Daumier had several styles. We can detect the influence of Rubens, on the one hand, of Fragonard on the other. We know that he made a copy of Rubens' *Kermesse*, which was destroyed in a fire. As for Fragonard, it is very likely that he saw drawings and engravings by that artist at the home of Alexandre Lenoir.

As always when portraying the effects of hard physical work, Daumier's tone becomes serious. Here we have another of those washerwomen he most often treated in dark tones, more rarely, as here, in full light, modeling her in bright colors.

He treated the same subject in sculpture, but his conception of sculptural form has never been brought out more clearly than in this painting. The basketful of laundry, still wringing wet, is so heavy that the woman cannot carry it in her arms. She has propped it against her hip, both arms holding it up like a belt, her hands coming together as the buckle. The weight is thus distributed over the entire body, bent forward and to her left with a powerful twist of the upper part.

The full light lingers over the laundry in the basket and the woman's shoulder. The long brush strokes are reminiscent of Fragonard's technique in certain works.

The woman's face expresses worry, haste, fatigue—all rendered with admirable economy of means. There is no literary declamation: everything is rendered in strictly pictorial terms. And we have met the little boy before who is clinging to his mother's skirt, trotting along like a young animal at her side, straining his short legs to keep up. The landscape is grandiose and, for all its brightness, a little sinister. From the opposite bank the city, like some immense white rock, keeps impassive watch while toiling humans go about fulfilling their destiny.

Painted about 1860

THE FIRST DIP *(Le Premier Bain)*

Oil on wood, $9^1/_2 \times 12^5/_8$"

Lower left corner: h. D.

Collection Oscar Reinhart, Winterthur, Switzerland

As we have said, Daumier rarely displayed interest in children. And yet in some of his works he reveals an unexpected tenderness for their blurred forms and uncertain movements. We even have a watercolor by him showing a group of three peasant babies playing in the care of their slightly older sister.

It is true that Daumier knew what it was to be a father, however briefly—just long enough, apparently, to show something of a father's feelings. He married a young seamstress, Alexandrine Dassy, on April 16, 1846, thus legalizing a relationship that had begun in 1842, perhaps even as early as 1839. On February 2, 1846, she had given birth to a son who was registered under the name of Honoré Daumier. What became of this son? He probably died very young, for we find no further mention of him. Conceivably, such a composition as this one preserves some faint echo of the father's experience.

The scene is the country in summer, probably at Valmondois—Daumier moved to a house there in 1865. The mother is a peasant. Her crouching position, as well as the form of the child whose first hesitant steps into the water she is guiding, bring to mind Millet. Daumier comes very close here to Millet in respect to both subject and coloring. Air and light play a great part in this type of painting, and in this respect it is all but Impressionist. Observe the bright area around the head and the dark hair of the standing girl in blue. Such effects of contrast were to become one of the essential elements of Seurat's art a few years after Daumier's death.

Painted about 1860–62

THE HORSEMEN *(Les Cavaliers)*

Oil on canvas, 25⁵/₈ × 33¹/₂"

Museum of Fine Arts, Boston

On the Ile Saint-Louis there are several famous stately old residences which were built in the seventeenth century, when the nearby quarter known as the "Marais" was still elegant. In Daumier's day the Ile, no longer fashionable, was inhabited chiefly by artists and humble folk. From his windows Daumier could see a bank of the Seine where horses were being brought all day to be watered. Often a stableboy would ride one of them without a saddle, leading two or three horses by the bridle. Sometimes the horses became restive and refused to leave the water. Daumier loved to watch all this. He claimed that he was unable to draw from nature, and this was true. But his extraordinary visual memory infallibly recorded the modifications of volumes in motion, and he retained the most characteristic, most synthesizing features of the movement. This is why paintings like the one shown here are far more lifelike and intensely animated than any photograph could be. The most amazing portion, perhaps, is the dark-colored horse: the way it shakes its mane, the way it sits back on its hocks, and, above all, the way Daumier has rendered its balking and the play of its muscles with a series of rapid white lines streaked across the glossy black coat.

In Géricault the nineteenth century had already had a great painter of horses (in Gros too, but above all in Géricault). Daumier certainly knew Géricault's horses, which Delacroix also greatly admired.

120

Painted about 1860–62

THE WATERING PLACE *(Baignade à l'Abreuvoir)*

Oil on wood, 17¹/₂ × 21¹/₂"

Lower right corner: h. D.

National Museum of Wales, Cardiff

Daumier liked to go for long leisurely walks, but all the time he lived on the Ile Saint-Louis he rarely covered any great distance (apart from his visits to Millet at Barbizon). He was no dandy, fond of the boulevards and famous *cafés* of the period, such as the Café Anglais or the fashionable terrace of the Tortoni. The sights he saw on the Ile Saint-Louis where he lived amply satisfied his need for observation and meditation. Only a stone's throw away, a little arm of the Seine lined with *bateaux-lavoirs* and places where horses were watered continually provided him with subjects. Gustave Geoffroy has left a fine description of this stretch of the Seine where Daumier could see "the horses being watered, solid work animals, looking like massive sculptures as they came up out of the water." The latent sculptor in Daumier would hardly have been drawn to expensive pedigreed breeds such as would catch the eye of Toulouse-Lautrec a few years later, or to the slender race horses whose lightness was so well rendered by Degas. He liked to paint Percherons, heavy draft horses, snorting as they drink.

But Daumier is essentially a classic painter. Daumier's classical training is forever cropping up, never more self-evidently than in his habit of seeing human beings first and foremost as nudes—what the studios at one time called "academically." We may be sure that the stableboys who took their horses down to the river wore their working clothes, but Daumier saw through to the "classical" constants under the realistic appearances. What he sees in the man on the horse in this work, more or less consciously, is no more nor less than what one of the sculptors of Trajan's Column would have seen. This half-naked rider on his sturdy horse startled by a dog barking takes on, under Daumier's brush, a grandiose quality. The group of horse and rider is built up out of a very few ample forms and becomes a kind of equestrian statue.

Painted about 1860–62

THE WASHERWOMAN *(La Lavandière)*

Oil on wood, 19¹/₄ × 13"

Lower right corner: h. D.

The Louvre, Paris

From where Daumier lived, at 9 Quai d'Anjou, he could see buildings on the opposite bank of the Seine rising like a scraggy cliff. Right underneath his window, on the near bank, were moored some of those *bateaux-lavoirs*—covered barges which served as community washhouses—the very last of which were still in existence not many years ago. Here women bustled about all day amid the racket of the paddles. At sunset they climbed up from the river's edge, bent under the weight of bundles of wet laundry. These women, who often brought their children with them for the day, inspired many of Daumier's paintings and sculptures. In his treatment of children, Daumier kept a classical attitude: for him they were creatures of physical and intellectual immaturity, not especially interesting in themselves.

Here, however, great tenderness is expressed in the way the mother leans protectively over the child; her right arm and helping hand are beautifully drawn. Daumier lovingly renders the physical effort of the child clutching the paddle and clambering up steps that are too high for him.

The execution of this painting is a tour de force. The mother and child, seen against the brilliant light of the buildings in the distance, are modeled in very dark tones, from the lower end of the color keyboard; and in them are marvelously rich flashes—blue in the child's clothes, the ruddy tones in the mother's skirt. Note also, under the mother's left hand, a shimmering spark of blue. These bright touches amid so somber and deep a chiaroscuro show that, if Daumier made a serious study of such an eighteenth-century artist as Fragonard, nonetheless his meditations in the Louvre had taught him also to revere another genius—Rembrandt. His affinities with this painter are particularly obvious here.

The background, vigorously brushed, is nevertheless modulated with exquisite delicacy. The warm, light tones are made brighter and richer by the contrast of the dark forms of the woman's body. For all its seeming effortlessness and quickness of observation, this painting encompasses countless pictorial subtleties.

Painted about 1860–62

MAN ON A ROPE *(L'Homme à la Corde à Nœuds)*

Oil on canvas, $44^1/_2 \times 28^3/_8''$

Museum of Fine Arts, Boston

Seeing a drawing by Daumier, Balzac exclaimed, "This fellow's got some of Michelangelo's guts!" It is one more evidence of Balzac's wonderful intuition where works animated by strong human feeling are concerned. Indeed, in this painting based on observation of a workman hoisting himself high above the ground, Daumier gave deeply felt expression to the epic quality of human labor.

It is among the awesome figures of the Sistine Chapel, no doubt, that we must look for the ultimate ancestor of this man climbing a rope. Daumier saw right through the work clothes to the classic nude. This work reinforces our belief—a belief already voiced by Raymond Escholier—that Daumier must have studied the great ancient sculptures in The Louvre. Alexandre Lenoir, a scholar of broad interests and a great admirer of antiquity, may well have influenced him along these lines.

In *Man on a Rope* the dislocation of the hip, the stiffness of the right leg, the bulging muscles of the right forearm, all go back to the Graeco-Roman world, but as we see it through Michelangelo's eyes. Hanging in mid-air like this, man is alone with his fate. Behind him is a steep wall, and at one side, the sky. As for the execution itself, it is of extraordinary directness. The colors overflow the contours to give the impression of a body swinging in the void.

We are reminded of Victor Hugo's lines in *Les Burgraves*, about men on their way to storm a walled town: "*...moins hommes que démons que le vent et la nuit tordaient au flanc des monts.*" ("...not so much men as demons, whom the night and the wind were twisting over the steep hillsides.")

126

Painted about 1860–65

FIVE SPECTATORS *(Spectateurs au Théâtre)*

Watercolor, $7^1/_2 \times 10^5/_8''$

Lower right corner: h. D.

Private collection, Paris

Color plays a far more important part in this work than in Daumier's other water-colors. Furthermore, the work is fairly exceptional in its stress on feminine charms, not normally a preoccupation with this artist. Virtually nothing we know about Daumier suggests that he ever experienced a great love. In the known letters he wrote to Alexandrine Dassy, first his mistress and later his wife, he called her "my Didine," and occasionally *"ma Négresse"* ("black beauty"). Such terms of endearment rather evoke a nursemaid's hearty kisses.

In this watercolor, however, we find a more complex attitude, possibly hinting at secret longings. In front of the two fashionable ladies, who are elegant enough but cold and unattractive, we are shown a somewhat langorous girl or young woman. The face, given in one-quarter view, has a lovely curving line; her cheek is smooth, the neck supple and unwrinkled. From her emanates an innate grace which, we feel, Daumier must have gazed at lovingly.

Her dewy freshness brings to mind Musset's lines inspired by a girl seated a few rows in front of him at the Théâtre Français: "... *un cou blanc, délicat se penche et de la neige effacerait l'éclat.*" (... a white delicate neck leans sidewise, more dazzling than glistening snow.")

Painted about 1862

THE THIRD-CLASS CARRIAGE
(Le Wagon de Troisième Classe)

Oil on wood, $10^1/_4 \times 13^3/_8''$

Lower right: h. Daumier

Collection Mr. and Mrs. David Bakalar, Boston

Daumier found a rich source of inspiration in the railroads, which he began to use in his work about 1855. At that time, trains were already reaching speeds of as much as fifty miles an hour, to the marvel of contemporaries. For some time now the train compartments, in which passengers who most often did not know one another sat face to face, had supplied a theme for humor. The caricaturist Henri Monnier, among others, liked to make up funny conversations, loaded with banalities, between chance acquaintances on trains.

Monnier and Daumier saw each other frequently between 1855 and 1860. Monnier made a portrait of Daumier, and Daumier one of Monnier, the latter perhaps intended as a frontispiece for Monnier's book, *The Memoirs of Joseph Prudhomme.* (Prudhomme is the archetypal middle-class Frenchman; pro-government, solemn, and stupid.) It may well be that Monnier suggested to his friend that he could find material in the humorous features of railway travel. However, it is noteworthy that among Daumier's numerous paintings, drawings, and watercolors on this theme, by no means all are intended to provoke laughter, though a few are very amusing. Portraying well-to-do passengers in first class (fig. 46), for example, his unsparing rendering of their sullen dignity is not humorous. He is more friendly toward passengers in second class—he often shows them yawning or dozing—but most sympathetic to third-class passengers. These are people of modest means, and he feels closest to them.

Not fond of traveling himself, he did however ride trains—for instance, in 1849 he took his wife to Langrune, a small watering place on the Channel. And he took the train when he went to see his friends Théodore Rousseau and Millet at Barbizon.

In the painting reproduced here, the relaxed pose of the patient man seated between the two peasant women is perfectly drawn; the woman and the child at the right are shown in a very sharp light, which is at the same time skillfully nuanced.

Painted about 1862

THE THIRD-CLASS CARRIAGE
(Le Wagon de Troisième Classe)

Oil on canvas, 25³/₄ × 35¹/₂"

The Metropolitan Museum of Art, New York. Bequest of Mrs. H. O. Havemeyer, 1929.

The H. O. Havemeyer Collection

This painting is rather exceptional among Daumier's works, in both its genesis and its technique. For a long time Daumier found it hard to sell his paintings and watercolors. When he painted for his own pleasure, he would sketch in the work very broadly, and then often put it aside in a corner of his studio, working at it again as the fancy took him. When it was finished, he would say, "I did the whole thing in two days." When he decided he had adequately expressed his feeling at the first try, he would leave the painting as it was. But now and again a prospective purchaser would ask for a more "finished" painting. In such a case Daumier would resign himself to a great deal of preliminary work; he would make line drawings, square up his sketches, transfer them to the canvas, and only then begin painting. Such was the case with the work reproduced here. He made at least two sketches for it, and in the course of execution, considered departures from them.

Here the precision and emphasis of the drawing is outstanding—in the hands and body of the peasant woman with the sleeping child in her arms, for example. So careful a treatment, resembling the engraver's, indicates the domination of the preliminary drawing or traced design that has come down to us. However, this treatment in no wise diminished the artist's sensibility or power. The light comes in through the carriage doors; the passengers at the right are in a penumbra of the sort Daumier excels at rendering. We have the impression that we can almost hear the rumbling of the train, which drowns out the voices of the passengers. The figures are vigorously "typed," their characters are made clear by their physical attitudes. The old peasant woman sits up straight, a trifle stiffly. The big-bosomed young woman with the child in her arms is entirely relaxed, half-asleep. The little boy dozing at the right is about to let his head fall gently against the old woman.

Painted about 1862–65

MOUNTEBANKS' SIDESHOW
(Parade de Saltimbanques)

Oil on canvas, $9^7/_8 \times 12^5/_8''$

Lower left corner: h. Daumier

Private collection, Paris

One day, after Daumier's death, someone mentioned his name to Forain, the humorist whose pitiless drawings and cruel captions were much appreciated by the Parisians. Forain replied, "Ah, Daumier! He was very different from us: he had heart."

The fact is, whenever Daumier portrays people who are poor and whose lives are insecure, he exhibits great compassion and fellow feeling. Nothing aroused these feelings in him more than traveling players, whose possessions amount to no more than what they stand up in and can carry with them: a rickety chair, a drum, a tattered rug, a not very fresh clown's costume. The life of such people inspired some of Daumier's most moving works, like the one reproduced here.

The scene is a little village. The central figure is wearing a Pierrot costume; his hat was in this period the standard clown's headgear. (Daumier often put it on the head of M. Thiers when he caricatured the future president of the Third Republic.) He is beating the drum to get the mistrustful, penny-pinching country people to come closer so his little family can put on their show. The woman is seated in a posture eloquent of weariness and dejection. A boy in acrobat's tights is spreading out a rug on which he will, perhaps, perform his own act a little later. Even more dramatic is the somewhat older boy standing at the left, thin, already matured by this hard life, looking at the group of peasants in the middle distance. They'd better make up their minds to come closer.... And if they do, then they'd better not all slink away when the hat is passed or there won't be much to eat this evening....

In this painting Daumier varied his technique. The group of peasants in the distance is rendered by simple contrasts of light and shadow. The entire foreground, on the other hand, is "written," as though with a pen. Line drawing here serves as chiaroscuro, with marvelous eloquence. The simple outline of the standing youth's profile, the short, trenchant line indicating the neck tendon, play their part in making this little painting an unforgettable masterpiece.

134

Painted about 1863

THE CHESS PLAYERS *(Joueurs d'Échecs)*

Oil on wood, 9⅝ × 12¾"

Lower left corner: h. Daumier

Musée du Petit-Palais, Paris

Daumier's life seems to have been a very busy one. When we learn of the newspaper offices that waited impatiently for his lithographs, and when we count all the friends around him for most of his life, we are likely to assume that this must have been as he wanted it to be. Looking at his works more closely, however, it seems possible that Daumier put up with this kind of life rather than chose it for himself. He was by nature an idler, whose circumstances were always such that he had to keep busy. He would have liked to be lazy, but life wouldn't let him. When Théodore de Banville kept after him to make a drawing for the masthead of a projected newspaper, *Le Corsaire*, Daumier confessed, "I'll work from morning to night when I have to, but at bottom I am more torpid than a snake in the sunshine...." Works like the one here, in which we see two chess players sitting in wordless absorption, probably in the back room of some little *café*, let him at least contemplate the peace and quiet he dreamed of. He also painted people playing cards and checkers.

Jean Adhémar has suggested that Daumier was attracted to such subjects by the literary model of Henri Monnier, whose comedy *The Painter and the Bourgeois* (1855) revolves around a game of dominoes. This is quite possible, but there are many works by Daumier which, like this one, reflect what I believe to be a need for peace and quiet—the figures in such works are not necessarily playing games.

This little painting is well-nigh sculptural, thanks to Daumier's skillful handling of the play of light. The hands, as expressive as the faces, are drawn with amazing truth and power. The hesitation of the player whose turn it is to make a move, and whose puzzled face is so strongly modeled in full light, and the waiting pose of the player in the shadow prove that a great artist can disclose the inner life of his figures by plastic means.

136

Painted about 1863–66

LUNCH IN THE COUNTRY *(Fin d'un Déjeuner)*

Oil on panel, 10 × 13¹/₈"

National Museum of Wales, Cardiff

A luncheon party out of doors. It is a good rendering of the relaxed mood of such a gathering; Madame Daumier felt somewhat intimidated on occasions such as when she accompanied her husband on visits to his friends Théodore Rousseau and Millet at Barbizon. It is a quick study, a few brush strokes sufficing to outline the figures and distribute the lights felicitously.

As always with Daumier, movement is expressed with amazing accuracy. The figures are probably portraits, especially the fully lighted figure at the left. The whites of the shirt front have been laid on very generously, with an almost creamy effect; there is a play of cold tones, underneath which appear several warm tones, notably at the left shoulder and on the right arm.

Daumier composed this study directly in color, as he might have treated the same subject in clay. Broad luminous brush strokes define the lifelike movement of the man at the center, shown lifting his cup to his mouth. It would seem, however, that there was a falling off in the artist's interest in his subject when he came to paint the figure at the right. To be sure, this figure, seen from the back and entirely in shadow, still presents a highly varied play of colors, but the drawing is less sharp, and the body under the clothes is less vividly suggested. We may also note the very luminous brush stroke over the dark-brown hair of the figure at the left, which forms a sort of halo and provides a powerful contrasting tone.

138

Painted about 1863–66

THE TROUBADOUR *(Le Troubadour)*

Oil on canvas, $30^3/_4 \times 22^1/_8''$

Lower right: h. D.

The Cleveland Museum of Art. Leonard C. Hanna, Jr., Collection

Daumier, who had a classical training in art and a sense of humor, never went in for romantic sentimentality. When Victor Hugo's play *Les Burgraves* failed in 1843, he made a lithograph showing the Muse of the Classical Theatre (Ponsard's very academic *Lucrèce* was just then a resounding success) casually routing with her foot a whole band of furious little burgraves.

Now, in Daumier's day, the "troubadour" style dominated the trappings of middle-class life. Music, the arts, and literature vied with one another in celebrating the more dramatic love stories of the Middle Ages and the Italian Renaissance.

In January, 1869, a one-act play in verse entitled *Le Passant* had an immense success. It was set in Florence at the time of Botticelli, and its author, François Coppée, became famous overnight. Its hero was a high-minded young troubadour like the one portrayed here. I can hardly believe that Daumier really enjoyed painting such a work, and am rather inclined to suspect that it was a subject he was asked to treat by a collector. Certainly he did not dash it off: the British Museum owns a study in black pencil which is a preliminary sketch for this figure.

Painted about 1863–66

THE AMATEUR TRIO *(Trio d'Amateurs)*

Oil on wood, $8^5/_8 \times 9^7/_8''$

Lower right corner: h. Daumier

Musée du Petit-Palais, Paris

The seriousness with which these two elderly men are singing to the violin accompaniment of a third might suggest that Daumier was a music lover. Unfortunately this was not the case, according to Banville. Daumier cared only for sentimental ballads, though he was amused by their insipidity. Switzerland was in this period very much in fashion; it was the place where couples went on their honeymoons. Banville tells us that Daumier used to hum a verse by Kettly, which describes the happiness of the natives of Switzerland at inhabiting "the happy land where Lavater saw the light of day," and where, "far from the city's trouble and woe," you breathe in great draughts of the fresh mountain air.

He did not at all appreciate Wagner (he pronounced it "*Vagnière*"), and the Pilgrims' Chorus from *Tannhäuser* seemed trash to him. But for all his personal indifference to music, in this painting Daumier is respectful of the three musicians' serious absorption in their art. He was always moved by genuine enthusiasm; moreover, these are not upper-class snobs but ordinary Frenchmen, the kind of men he had met on the barricades. Still, Daumier's primary interest in this trio is the opportunity it offers him to display his gifts as a painter and sculptor. The heads are modeled with extraordinary power and sureness. The nose of each of the two singers is given its individual form in a single brush stroke; the forehead of the violinist is placed full in the light with a single application of paint.

The Daumier who could caricature M. Thiers over and over again with inexhaustible verve was also capable of quiet concentration. Works such as this one perhaps bring us closest to his true nature.

142

Painted about 1863–66

TWO SCULPTORS *(L'Atelier d'un Sculpteur)*

Oil on wood, 11 × 14"

The Phillips Collection, Washington, D. C.

Here is a work which, we feel sure, Daumier painted for his own pleasure, on one of those small wood panels he was so fond of using. The temperament of a born sculptor is here most clearly revealed. The figures are treated just as if he had shaped them in clay. To endow their attitude with density, to make us share their wordless attention to the piece of sculpture, all he needed was large spots of light contrasting with the deep but differentiated shadow in which the studio is bathed. Their expressions are strikingly absorbed. The more heavily bearded man, obviously the maker of the little sculpture they are examining, is probably the sculptor Clésinger (who had been politically active under the Republic of 1848). He is going over his work, perhaps looking for some defect, something to alter. The other man is watching attentively, head tilted slightly, in a way that makes us share his interest.

In this simple yet lively sketch Daumier said, very quickly and straight off, everything he had to say. The concentrated attention of the two men against the penumbra dramatizes Daumier's conception of artistic creation as imbued with a kind of religious solemnity. There is deep and melancholy nobility in such a work. "Melancholy" because there was around the studios then a saying, "Oh you poor man—you're a *sculptor!*" In the age of that art's decline, it is not hard to imagine these two men discussing in hushed voices the fate of Antoine Moine, Préault's great friend (and thus also Daumier's), who, penniless, killed himself in 1849, at the age of fifty-eight.

Painted about 1866

MOUNTEBANKS RESTING
(Saltimbanques au Repos)

Oil on canvas, $21^{1}/_{4} \times 24^{3}/_{8}''$

Lower left corner: h. Daumier

Collection Mr. and Mrs. Norton Simon, Fullerton, California

Daumier made many paintings of circus and carnival people—in this he followed a tradition going back to the eighteenth century. Writers of the Romantic era also exploited this milieu, but they most often treated it in a sentimental mood; their favorite figure was Pagliacci, the clown who makes people laugh while his heart is breaking. Baudelaire's prose poem, *The Old Clown* (published in 1862), which Daumier certainly knew, still reflects this melancholy, nostalgic vein. Daumier, however, is rarely sentimental, and there are very few lovers (happy or unhappy) in his pictures. If he himself ever knew the pangs of unrequited love he never confided them to anyone, especially not in his paintings and drawings. What catches his eye in circus or carnival people, most often, is the contrast between their conspicuously lively, even frenzied expenditure of energy "out front," entertaining the public, and their slumping weariness backstage once the show is over. The contrast is most marked where, as here, they are still in make-up and costumes.

After Daumier, such twentieth-century painters as Derain and Picasso were also moved sympathetically by this theme. The painting reproduced here shows carnival entertainers counting their takings. One of them, in Pierrot costume, sits across from a fellow artist who is stacking coins. In the foreground, his back toward the viewer, is a youth in acrobat's tights. Daumier more than once rendered such boys, still children almost, but already matured by the hardships and instability of the traveling players' life. We can all but see the bodies of the men under the loose drapery of their costumes. Pierrot's white clown's suit seems woven of tones delicately varied according to the angle of the light that falls on it. The man counting the money wears a reddish costume that stands out against the dark background of the shed or wagon they are sitting in. Here supreme pictorial skill joins with the artist's conception of his theme and his sympathy with it to produce a great painting.

146

Painted about 1866

THE WRESTLERS *(Les Lutteurs)*

Oil on wood, 16¹/₂ × 10⁵/₈"

Lower left corner: h. Daumier

The Ordrupgaard Collection, Copenhagen

This painting belonged to Daubigny; there is a preliminary study for it at the Albertina Museum in Vienna. It is often held to be one of Daumier's earliest paintings, and this may well be true. The brush strokes are not as free nor the drawing as vigorous as in the works we admire more, such as *Man on a Rope* (page 127).

Daumier was inspired here by the most popular sport of his day—Graeco-Roman wrestling, also called "flat-hand wrestling." The fists could not be used, and the only holds permitted were between the neck and the waist. Southern France had its local champions. A novel by Cladel entitled *Ompdrail, le Tombeau des Lutteurs*, telling the tale of a famous southern wrestler's life, was a best-seller. Gavarni made an attractive drawing of one of the champions of the amateur wrestling which was practiced in the Paris suburbs. At the Salon of 1853, Courbet exhibited a painting (which shocked the public) showing two wrestlers in action; Daumier certainly saw it. The vogue for this sport lasted until about 1925. At country fairs throughout France, wrestlers had booths of their own and took on all challengers—the most famous was the "Marseilles" booth.

Here Daumier shows the sort of match which held crowds spellbound in his day. The group of two wrestlers in the lighted ring is drawn firmly, in emphatic outline. Most remarkable, however, is the way Daumier has modeled the large figure in the foreground, almost exclusively in variations of warm tones (the shoulder, a portion of the left thigh) and cold tones (almost the whole right side of the body). To be noted also is a curious "echo" of the red curtain on his right forearm. Daumier's technique here is already quite "impressionistic."

148

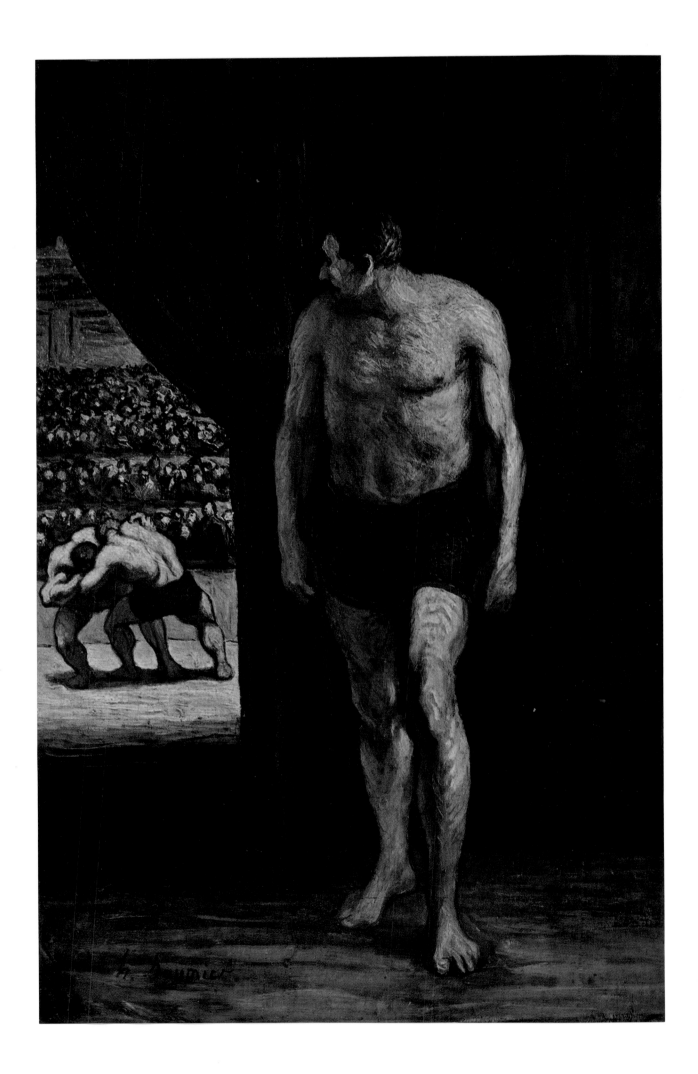

Painted about 1866

DON QUIXOTE ATTACKING THE WINDMILLS *(Don Quichotte Chargeant les Moulins)*

Oil on canvas, 22 × 33¹/₈″

Lower left corner: h. Daumier

Collection Mr. and Mrs. Charles S. Payson, New York

It was probably about 1850 that Daumier began what may be called his *Don Quixote* cycle. Together these works are very revealing of his innermost self, materializations, as it were, of his own aspirations. Daumier was a lucid observer of his age, however, and here it is the faithful Sancho who bears distressed witness to the wildly impractical idealism of the Knight of the Doleful Countenance.

The theme of Don Quixote seems to have freed Daumier technically. His drawing now carries freedom of form to the point of frenzy. In the studios it was customary to contrast Daumier's drawings with those of Ingres, the most amazing interpreter of form who had ever lived. But real art lovers were even then aware that there was no fundamental opposition between the two. As early as 1841 an article in *Le Charivari* spoke of Ingres and Daumier as "the Siamese twins of beauty," worthy representatives of "complete art." Baudelaire, in turn, spoke of Ingres and Daumier as the two great draftsmen of the century. And since Baudelaire also detected profound affinities between Ingres and Courbet, for all their obvious incompatibilities, we may say that Ingres, Courbet, and Daumier were the three finest draftsmen the century could pride itself upon.

In the painting shown here, the action is strongly expressed both plastically and psychologically: in the foreground the sensible Sancho wrings his hands in despair at the spectacle of his master charging off wildly on some disastrous expedition. Don Quixote is headed across the plain, drunk with the sublime madness that makes him tilt at windmills.

Painted about 1868

DON QUIXOTE

Oil on canvas, 18¹/₈ × 12⁵/₈"

Lower right corner: h. D.

Neue Pinakothek, Munich

If we judged merely by outward appearances, we would have to conclude that Daumier was the most sociable of men. On the Ile Saint-Louis he lived next door to the old Hôtel Lauzun, where Baudelaire occupied an attic and where the painter Boissard de Boisdenier kept an elegant apartment on a lower floor. The latter was a meeting place for the elite of Paris in art and letters, and Daumier was received with open arms.

During the years he was in disfavor (1860 to 1864) and *Le Charivari* did not print his drawings, Daumier lived in Montmartre. His friends lost track of him during this time and worried about what might have happened to him. But in 1864 *Le Charivari* made due apology to the artist and asked him to contribute regularly again. This provided occasion for a triumphal banquet.

At Valmondois, where he moved permanently in 1865 (without, however, giving up his lodgings in Montmartre, which he kept until his death), he was surrounded by the affectionate attentions of Daubigny, Geoffroy Dechaume, and Corot. Corot, as fond of the man as respectful of the artist, would have but two paintings in his bedroom—the portrait of his mother, and one of Daumier's lawyers.

And yet ... some of Daumier's works seem to disclose a tormenting desire to escape. A real thirst for silence and solitude occasionally breaks through with extraordinary intensity. Several versions of *Don Quixote* include the faithful Sancho, but here Don Quixote is off into the desert on his own, a weird ghost of a man on a nightmarish horse, without bridle or stirrups, the bones sticking out of its skin. The disembodied hero has even lost his face. The drawing and the colors (which, however, are fused) in this strange, grandiose, symbolic work aroused the enthusiasm of Vincent van Gogh. In 1882 he wrote his brother Théo: "Yes, indeed, it is possible that Daumier was the teacher of us all."

Painted about 1868

DON QUIXOTE AND THE DEAD MULE

Oil on wood, $9^3/_4 \times 18^1/_8$"

Lower left corner: h. D.

The Metropolitan Museum of Art, New York. Wolfe Fund, 1909

Though quite small in size, this work gives the impression of being monumental. The light, coming from the right, spreads across wildly broken ground, like a stream bed. This is not a landscape of sand and ashes, as is the big sketch in Zurich. It is a narrow passage between tumbled earth and rocks. The first rays of the morning sun fall across the hero's mount and spill in a tragic pool of light just in front of the dead mule. The lighting effects are theatrical. The dead animal bars Don Quixote's way—he stands spotlighted in the distance. Daumier leads the eye toward him with all the skill of a stage director. The disquieting loneliness of the place, the silence broken only by Rosinante's clumsy hoofs, the light that draws Don Quixote's attention toward the lifeless beast, the shadows cast along the rough trail—all this makes the painting a wordless drama, the seeming tranquillity of the scene shot through with nervous tensions. Technically, the painting is rich, sweeping, sure. By a skillful contrasting effect, the dark body of the dead mule is at once haloed and yet made more inert.

Daumier was fascinated with this theme of the encounter between Don Quixote and the dead mule. He painted it again as a mural decoration in his friend Daubigny's studio at Auvers.

Painted about 1869

IN A PAINTER'S STUDIO
(Dans l'Atelier d'un Peintre)

Oil on canvas, 12¹/₄ × 9⁷/₈"

Collection Mr. and Mrs. Norton Simon, Fullerton, California

Here the sculptor in Daumier, who puts shadows in convex surfaces and high-lights points of relief, also makes use of the shimmering *fa presto* effects that Fragonard employed with such mastery. This was one of the times when Daumier's customary indifference to feminine attractions gave place to real feeling, to something like rapture at the sight of a young woman's bare shoulder, the curve of her full-fleshed arm, the tilt of her charming head.

Daumier, it has often enough been said, never cut the figure of the sentimental lover. However, there may have been one amorous episode in his life, apart from his marriage. A friend of his relates in *Le Charivari* for July 21, 1839, in a bantering tone, that Daumier fell in love with a young Englishwoman he saw at the Brasserie Anglaise. According to this account, she went back to England before he was able to declare his admiration for her. An issue of the *Journal de Dimanche* in 1845 contains another story. Someone asked Daumier why his lithographs so often showed the features of a particular woman (treated comically). "You are reviving my grief, "Daumier answered. "It is the portrait of a woman I loved very much." "Is she pretty?" "Yes, in the daguerreotype."

Was this supposed to be facetious? Or just a way of evading a prying question? It is hard to tell with Daumier. At all events, in the work reproduced here the sincerity of his feelings is undeniable. The mastery with which he ruffles and fluffs out the drapery with a single stroke of the brush brings Fragonard to mind.

Painted about 1869

PIERROT STRUMMING THE GUITAR
(Pierrot Chantant)

Oil on canvas, $13^3/_8 \times 10^1/_4''$

Lower left corner: h. D.

Collection Oscar Reinhart, Winterthur, Switzerland

This is a work in which the brush has run over the surface at top speed, without
hesitating or pausing for corrections. It is a symphony of lights, utterly impromptu
in character, a play of very pale whites just tinged with yellow, blue, and lake.
Jean Adhémar has pointed out analogies between this painting, so rapid, so fresh
in its harmonies, and certain paintings by Fragonard. He recalls that in 1869
Daumier greatly admired certain eighteenth-century works which The Louvre had
just acquired with the Lacaze collection, and that he often went there "to question
the old masters and study them," that he discussed them in long conversations.
Now, one of the jewels among the new acquisitions was *L'Étude*, a work Fragonard had composed very hurriedly, but with what brilliance! With respect both
to feeling and to technique, the analogies between this Fragonard and Daumier's
Pierrot Strumming the Guitar are too striking to be accounted for merely by vague
similarity of the temperaments of the two artists. On the other hand, this work was
painted ten years before Daumier died. Was not his failing eyesight already
troubling him? This may have induced him to apply a technique characterized
by broad, clear, legible strokes, whose interlacings could be grasped effortlessly
by the painter's tired eyes.

SELECTED BIBLIOGRAPHY

Daumier's life and work aroused the curiosity and admiration of many of his contemporaries—Baudelaire, Théodore de Banville, and Champfleury, among others. More recently, CLAUDE ROGER-MARX and JEAN CHERPIN (particularly in *Arts et Livres de Provence*, Marseilles, 1948) devoted a number of important studies to him which constitute a whole library in themselves.

The most complete work, which we have made constant use of in this book, is the one by JEAN ADHÉMAR, curator of the print department of the Bibliothèque Nationale, Paris (*Honoré Daumier*, published by Pierre Tisné, Paris, 1954). Among other works in which Daumier is treated exhaustively, the following may be mentioned:

GENERAL WORKS

ALEXANDRE, A. *H. Daumier, l'homme et l'œuvre*. Paris 1888.
BERTRAM, A. *H. Daumier*. London, 1929.
CASSOU, J. "Daumier l'homme des foules," *Arts de France* (1948), no. 21–22.
COURTHION, P. *Daumier raconté par lui-même et par ses amis*. Geneva, 1945.
ESCHOLIER, R. *Daumier: Peintre et lithographe*. Paris, 1923.
FONTAINAS, A. *La peinture de Daumier*. Paris 1923.
FOSCA, F. *Daumier*. Paris, 1933.
FUCHS, E. *Der Maler Daumier*. Munich, 1927. 2nd enlarged ed., 1930.
GOBIN, M. *Daumier, sculpteur (1808–1879)*. Geneva, 1953.
KLOSSOWSKI, E. *Honoré Daumier*. Munich, 1923.
LASSAIGNE, J. *Daumier*. Translated from French by E. B. Shaw. London, 1938.
LEJEUNE, R. *Daumier*. Munich, 1946.
LUTHER-CARY, E. *Honoré Daumier*. New York, 1907.
MARCEL, H. *H. Daumier: Biographie critique*. Paris, 1907.
REY, R. *Daumier*. Paris, 1923.

SADLER, M. *Daumier, the Man and the Artist*. London, 1923.
THACKERAY, W. M. *The Paris Sketch Book, by Mr. Titmarsh*. London, 1840; 1885 ed., pp. 192–226 (about Robert Macaire).
VALÉRY, P. *Degas, Manet, Morrisot*, pp. 155–160. (*Collected Works of Paul Valéry*, XII). New York, 1960.
VENTURI, L. *Modern Painters*, 2 vols. New York, 1947, 1950.

EXHIBITIONS

THE FREE LIBRARY, Philadelphia. *Lithographs and Drawings by Daumier Lent by Lessing J. Rosenwald*. 1930.
MUSEUM OF ART, Philadelphia. *Daumier 1808–1879*. 1937. Introduction by Claude Roger-Marx.
THE MUSEUM OF MODERN ART, New York. *Eighth Loan Exhibition: Corot, Daumier*. 1930. Introduction by Alfred H. Barr, Jr.
L'ORANGERIE, Paris. *Catalogue de l'exposition Daumier à l'Orangerie*. 1934.
THE ROSE ART MUSEUM, Waltham, Massachusetts. *Honoré Daumier ...Prints, Sculpture and Drawings*. Waltham, The Poses Institute of Fine Arts, 1963. Introduction by Alain de Leiris and Thomas H. Garver.
TATE GALLERY, London. *Daumier. Paintings and Drawings*. The Arts Council of Great Britain. 1961. Introductions by Alan Bowness and K. E. Maison.

REPRODUCTIONS

ADHÉMAR, J. *Honoré Daumier: Drawings and Watercolors*. (English ed.) New York and Basel, 1954.
DELTEIL, L. *Le Peintre-graveur illustré*, vols. 20–29: *Honoré Daumier*. Paris, 1926–1930.
LEMANN, B. *Honoré Daumier*. 240 lithographs. New York, 1946.
MAISON, K. E. *Daumier Drawings*. New York and London, 1960.
REY, R. *Honoré Daumier* (Pocket Library of Great Art). New York: Harry N. Abrams, 1959.